THE VILLAGE
HORSE DOCTOR:
West of the Pecos

Ben K. Green

THE VILLAGE HORSE DOCTOR:
West of the Pecos

CASTLE BOOKS

This edition published in 2005 by
CASTLE BOOKS ®
A division of Book Sales, Inc.
114 Northfield Avenue
Edison, NJ 08837

This edition published by arrangement with and permission of
ALFRED A. KNOPF
A division of Random House, Inc.
1745 Broadway
New York, New York 10019

Originally published May 19, 1971

Library of Congress Card Catalog Card Number: 79-118716

ISBN-13: 978-0-7858-2099-4
ISBN-10: 0-7858-2099-X

Printed in the United States of America

Howdy

*The Village Horse Doctor is an accurate
account of my true experiences during my years
of practice in the Far Southwest as the first
veterinary doctor at Fort Stockton, Texas.*

*I offer no apologies for having written the true
facts about the conditions in this desert country,
and I have the highest regard for a rugged breed
of people who were ever grateful for my efforts
and so charitable of my many mistakes.*

*My life has been rough but it has never been
dull and the time covered by these chapters is
probably the roughest and the furtherest from
being dull as any years that I have so far spent on
this earth.*

*You will find no bibliographies or other list of
references in this book since all the material is
that of the Village Horse Doctor himself.*

Ben K. Green

Contents

THE VILLAGE HORSE DOCTOR:
West of the Pecos

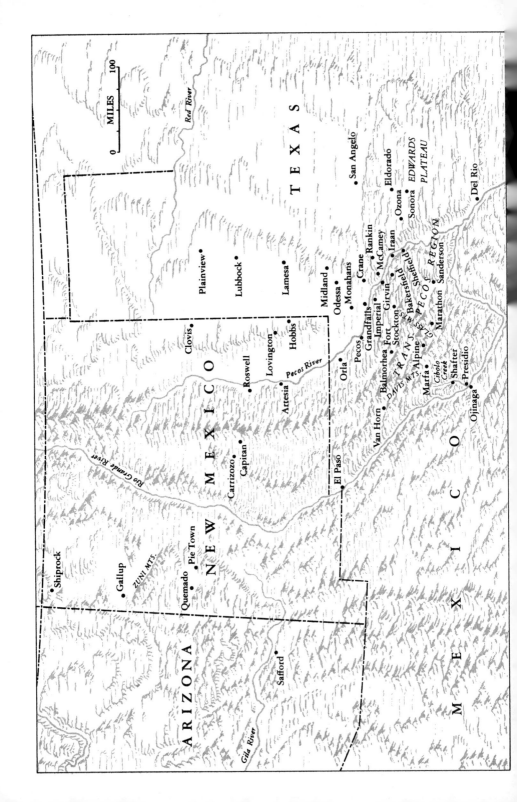

SMART?
HORSE DOCTOR

On January 4, 1944, I crossed the Pecos River between McCamey and Girvin headed for Old Mexico to practice veterinary medicine. It was midafternoon and a "blue norther" was blowin' down from the Rockies, and I could see heavy black clouds come rollin' down the Pecos River draw that were comin' off the Panhandle of Texas.

A few months earlier I had loaned a good two-door Dodge to some friends of mine. They got drunk and drove it under a truckload of wheat. My car was demolished and one of the boys was killed in the wreck. The Second World War was in full swing and buying a new car was next to impossible, so I got a used-car dealer to let me have the best he had.

It was a 1937 two-door Chevrolet with the usual story about havin' belonged to an old-maid schoolteacher who had never driven it over 20 mph and had never been off the pavement with it. A whole lot of this might have been so because the old car was in an excellent state of preservation, but I had it loaded with a year's supply of veterinary drugs and instruments and it wasn't eatin' up that desert road towards Mexico very fast.

It was dark when I pulled into Fort Stockton, Texas. The blizzard had struck and the temperature was falling fast. A day or two before, I had slammed the door on the right side of the car a little hard tryin' to push the overload back into it and had broken out about a fourth of the top of the glass in the door. This little opening was makin' me very much aware of the change in the weather, and I decided to check in at Fort Stockton for the night.

I registered at the Springhurst Hotel. It was too cold to loaf around and get acquainted with the town, so I ate a big supper in the dining room and sat around awhile in the lobby, which was quiet and peaceful. I visited with Benny Walker, who was the porter and after ten p.m. the porter and night clerk combined. We had a little light conversation. Benny was very well mannered and didn't pry into my business, and I didn't volunteer any information. After a while I walked upstairs and went to bed.

Early next morning I discovered that the Springhurst Hotel was the early-morning coffee shop for all the ranchers who lived in town and went to their ranches in the morning. They had begun to gather in the dining room, and, of course, the weather was the main topic of conversation. The temperature was down to 16 degrees above, and I gathered that this was an unusual spell for the dry Trans-Pecos Region of Texas.

Since I had been a cowboy all my life, nobody would have suspicioned from my appearance that I was a veterinary doctor, and nothing in their lingo seemed strange or unusual to me since I spoke their language too. During this early-morning session that I was stretchin' an ear out for, I heard the argument that the wind was puttin' up as it blew down the main street, which ran north and south, so I decided I would hole up here for a few days until the weather broke.

The next morning I was sittin' in the lobby watchin' the natives for pastime when a man walked over and introduced himself as Russell Payne. He was tall, light complexioned, and had a cigar that grew between his fingers and, when he stuck it in his mouth, gave off lots of smoke signals. He was a cowboy who had graduated to the livestock commission business and evidently was doing better at it than cowboy'n'.

After he learned that I was a veterinary doctor, he called to Alf TenyCke, Pat Cooper, Doug Adams, and several others who belonged in the coffee crowd as they came from the dining room into the lobby. As he introduced me to them, it seemed that it was the sudden thought of everybody that I should settle in the community.

The weather was bad and nobody was in a hurry, so we sat around the lobby stove, and they all put up a good talk about how much stock there was in the country and that it was a hundred and fifty miles or more in any direction to a vet. Of course, they all thought I would do real well there. I didn't discourage them too much and didn't make any sudden remarks about stayin', as I pretty well had my head set for Chihuahua City, Mexico.

The weather didn't break and ice stayed on the ground for sixteen days, which according to the natives was supposed to be some kind of record for freezing weather. During this time I had visited around the two drugstores. One, owned by Roger Gallemore, was on the west side of the main street on the north end of the block close to the bank. He and his wife, Ida, who everybody commonly referred to as Mrs. G, had been exceptionally nice to me and insisted that I settle in Fort Stockton.

Joe Henson operated the Stockton Pharmacy on the south corner of the same block. He, too, had offered much encouragement. Since the town was crowded because of the airfield and office space was next to impossible, both he and Gallemore had offered to take my calls and stock any kind of drugs that I would use.

Othro Adams was in the livestock commission and irrigation farming business. His office was in the Springhurst Hotel and opened off the back side of the lobby and onto a side street. Othro was a good operator and wanted me to stay in Fort Stockton and offered to share his office space with me. His particular interest was sheep and this was a big sheep country, and he asked in a very respectful manner, "Doctor, what do you know about sheep?"

"Well," I said, "I kept a thousand head of sheep for about five years in one of my ranching operations."

He kept a straight face, but his eyes laughed when he said, "If a man caught on slowly, he wouldn't learn much from just a thousand sheep in five years."

I had gotten acquainted with a lot of people in the sixteen days that the weather was bad but hadn't made any decision until I struck up a conversation in front of the

Stockton Pharmacy with an old rancher who was not particularly interested in the development of the country or the welfare of the livestock and had no concern for the success or well-being of his fellow man. His voice was toned pretty close to that of a bullfrog, his eyes were squinted, and from his dress, you would have assumed that his world's gatherings didn't amount to very much.

He said, "I seen you round here several days. What's yore business here?"

I told him that I was just passin' through and had stopped for the weather to fair up, that I had been headed for Chihuahua City to practice veterinary medicine. I said, however, that several people had suggested I set up practice in Fort Stockton.

He gave off a little mournful kind of sneerin' laugh and said, "This is healthy stock country and there's no business here for no horse doctor. What few times the country's had a die-out, there's always been enough cattle and sheep and horses left to restock in a few years. It's a pretty good place to live, if you can stand the people in it; and if you want to stay round, it wouldn't hurt nothin', but you might have to do some day-work on a chuck wagon durin' workin' times to make a livin' 'cause there ain't nobody in this country silly enough to pay somebody else to doctor a horse when they can do it themselves just as good as a horse doctor."

I thanked him for his advice and told him that he had made up my mind. As I walked off, he said, "I'm shore glad you listened and that yore goin' to move on. Us ranchers don't need nobody else to be livin' offn'em."

He didn't understand what I meant when I said he had made up my mind.

I moved to a motel up on the highway where I had more room to store my drugs and supplies and get them out of my car. In the sixteen days that I had been there, I had vaccinated one dog for rabies, and the going price for a small dog that didn't take much vaccine was $1.50. Up to now this had been my total practice.

For the next few days I put out the word that I had decided to stay, and I began to get a small amount of practice that I think could be termed "test practice." I took out a horse's tooth for Boyd Clayton and floated some horses' teeth for Fred Montgomery. For the rest of the month of January, I did some small chores for Alf TenyCke, Guy Rochell, John Bennett, and others that were just little things they had done in order to give me some practice and get me to stay. I knew this, however, and it showed a good attitude on the part of those who didn't need anything done on their livestock.

I hadn't gotten any kind of emergency call that would give me a chance to demonstrate my professional ability. However, during this same period, I had made some awful professional and conversational busts about the poisonous plants that were and had been killing off sheep during the winter ever since man had stocked this country with sheep, cattle, and goats.

One morning in the Stockton Pharmacy J. C. "Con" Cunningham was introduced to me and he immediately brought up the subject of yellowweed, and I told him frankly that I had never heard of it. Some other ranchers joined in the conversation and gave me a run-down on the history of yellowweed.

It is a grayish-green weed with lush, meaty-type leaves that comes in the dead of winter when there is nothing else green. As it matures, it has a large daisy-type bloom with a great excess of yellow pollen that will stain the wool on the face and legs of sheep that are grazing on the plant. Sheep by nature are weed-eaters and green-feeders and start eating yellowweed as soon as it is big enough to graze in the late fall and early winter. It was explained to me that the first sheep would die about ten to eleven days after they were put on yellowweed pasture, and unless you moved them, if the yellowweed was abundant enough, practically all would be dead in less than thirty days.

Mr. Cunningham stayed longer than the rest, and I, in spite of all my ignorance of these desert plants, immediately said, "It sounds simple to me, and I'll just give Mr. Henson back here a prescription for enough to treat a few sheep if you're interested."

His eyes brightened and a big smile crossed his face and he said, "Doctor, I'll be glad to try anything that you would prescribe."

We walked back to the prescription department and Mr. Cunningham briefed Joe Henson, the druggist, on what had transpired up at the fountain, and I said, "Yes, hand me a prescription blank."

I wrote out a prescription for enough medication to fill fifty sheep-size capsules and felt real smart. Mr. Cunningham said, "What do I owe you?"

I said, "Why don't you wait to see how much good we do the sheep?"

Joe looked the other way—I know now to hide his amusement, but at the time I didn't think about it. Mr. Cunningham said, "That's fair enough. I'm glad you're here."

As I walked away, I remarked, "If this don't do the job, I'll take a closer look at the sheep."

Little did I know how serious the death loss from yellowweed had been for the many years that sheep had been in the Trans-Pecos Region of Texas, and I had no idea how many people—doctors and others—had tried to treat yellowweed without success.

In a few days I saw Mr. Cunningham and asked about the sheep, and he said they seemed to be doing very well. I felt pretty good about this, so the next time I was in the drugstore, I asked Joe Henson, "Has Mr. Cunningham had the sheep prescription refilled?"

Nobody was around to listen and Joe, embarrassed for me as he was, endeavored to explain to me in a courteous manner that he told Mr. Cunningham that the prescription was too damn simple to do yellowweed any good and that they never had filled it the first time. This came as quite a blow to me; it was the first big, loud-mouthed mistake I had made in my first month in the Trans-Pecos Region.

During this same period of time, M. R. Gonzalez, who was a good citizen, with a grocery store, livestock, and other interests, had a bunch of sick hogs. M. R. had a contract with the airfield to haul the garbage, and he had a hog-feeding operation where he was feeding this garbage. He had gone to Roger Gallemore at the other drugstore for advice, and Roger hastened to inform him that they had a first-rate veterinary doctor who had just moved to Fort Stockton. M. R. was delighted when Roger called me to the back of the drugstore and introduced us.

He was glad to have my services, so we went to the south edge of town to look at his hogs. There were dead ones and some that were dying and some at the stage at which they were almost fat. There must have been about ninety head. The garbage for these hogs was being collected in iron barrels and the acid reaction was causing ferric poisoning; however, at the time I didn't know about the iron barrels, and in the last stages, all symptoms indicated that they were dying of swine erysipelas.

I did a post-mortem on several of these hogs that were dying and showed M. R. the indication of poisoning in the spleen and kidney, as well as the digestive tract. M. R. was a very pleasant heavy-set fellow, and he patted me on the back and said, "Doc-tor, you're sure smart. Now what do you want to do to save my hogs?"

I explained to him that I had the medicine to counteract the poisoning and we would go back to the drugstore and Gallemore would order the vaccine for erysipelas. This suited him fine and that afternoon we caught each one of the hogs and I gave them medicine by mouth.

The next day about the usual number had died, and I gave them more medicine.

The next day I had the vaccine that we had ordered, so we vaccinated them, and I gave more medicine by mouth. In about a week the number that were dying had slowed down, but the percentage was about the same—there were just fewer hogs.

M. R. was a good fellow and a real stayer and never complained, and we treated his hogs until they all died. This was my second bad case in my early practice in Fort Stockton.

One day later, M. R. told me, "Doc-tor, I sure like you and hope you come by to visit even if I don't have any hogs for you to kill."

An old man out in the edge of town on the irrigation ditch had a pet monkey that had a rash breaking out all over his body, and I really fixed him up. I gave him some medication and all his hair came off.

It seemed that I had done nothing right—my diagnoses were bad, my treatments were worse, and it was getting a little harder for the druggist to tell the people that there was a veterinary doctor in town. Well, I didn't feel too bad about the damn monkey because I didn't think I would have any large monkey practice in the Trans-Pecos Region of Texas.

Frank Smith, the druggist who worked for Roger Galle-

more, had a little mixed-breed pet dog that had recovered from distemper before I got there (otherwise he might not have recovered), but was seriously afflicted with chorea, which is a nervous disorder that is sometimes the aftermath of distemper in dogs and is generally considered incurable. The afflicted dog flinched, jerked, and twitched whether he was awake or asleep, so Frank asked me if I would "do away" with the dog. Well, this wasn't the kind of practice I had in mind either, but small-animal practice was going to be something that I couldn't avoid, so I consented to take care of this chore.

I took the little fellow in my car out in a pasture and gave him an extremely large intravenous injection of phenobarbitol, enough to have put a horse to sleep and left him layin' out in the weeds. In about three days he showed up at home very hungry and for some unexplainable reason, cured of his jerkin', twitchin' chorea. This little incident wasn't interpreted by the dog lovers of the community as a recommendation for me as a small-animal practitioner.

The cases that I have cited are by no means all the professional mistakes that I made, but it will show that I wasn't making a favorable impression on the region as an outstanding veterinary practitioner. By now I had begun to ponder the reasons for stopping in Fort Stockton, and I was thinkin' wistfully of Chihuahua, Mexico.

LECHUGUILLA

Early one morning I met Guy Rochell on the main block of town. He was a very pleasant and sociable kind of fellow who ranched about thirty-five miles south of Fort Stockton on the Sanderson road. He stopped me and we started a conversation.

He said he was driving out to his ranch for a little while and would be back about noon and asked me if I would care to go with him. Well, the demands for my services were far from pressing, and I didn't think I would be missed for any reason before noon, so I told him that it would be my pleasure to accompany him and see his ranch. By the tone of his voice, it seemed an afterthought when he said, "I'll call Mrs. Rochell to have a good dinner fixed for us when we get back."

As we started to leave town he said, "By the way, if you care to, we'll put your medicine bags in the back of my car in case you might need to have something with you when I show you some sick buck sheep."

As we drove along to the ranch, he told me about sheep eating lechuguilla. I had never heard of the plant, so I asked some rather sensible questions and listened carefully (I intended to profit from my yellowweed experience). Guy was an intelligent man with a lifetime of ranching experience and he explained very carefully all he knew about lechuguilla.

It is a dagger-like cactus plant that grows in the high rimrock and remote regions of the hills and is seldom eaten by sheep or goats until after cold weather. Then it seems that sheep will eat lechuguilla for the juice as well as the flavor and will not come in to water. Since this is a high fibrous diet, they will develop an impaction in the stomach, and in the carcasses of sheep that have died from lechuguilla, there will be balls of tightly compressed dried fiber that they have been unable to digest. After they are dead,

many times this ball of fiber will not decompose as quickly as the body of the sheep and will lay on the ground for years.

When sheep affected by lechuguilla were brought in from the ridges and placed in corrals with feed and water, they refused to eat or drink and the symptoms were what was commonly referred to as "dry mouth." Their lips would be sealed together with dried phlegm and their faces would swell, and their lips and noses, if they lived long enough, would peel off from the extreme temperature they had endured.

By the time Guy had finished his explanation and description, we drove up to a small chute pen where several of these bucks had been brought in and placed on feed and water. They had been there several days and had not eaten nor drank. I was very deliberate in my examination of these sheep and weighed carefully all the information that he had given me. I went to my medicine bags and prepared some hypodermic injections that I gave these several bucks.

This was about all we saw of the ranch and, I think, this was Guy's only intention when we left town. I don't believe it had occurred to him to do this until the moment he saw me that morning on the sidewalk. Three or four days passed and I hesitated to ask about the bucks fearful of a continuation of my recent experiences.

It was a cold morning and the average number of ranchers were holed up in the hotel lobby and drinking coffee in the dining room, and Guy motioned to me to come over to the table where he and some other ranchers were seated. I walked over—and by now I knew all of them—spoke and sat down. Guy volunteered the information to the rest of the men at the table that I had been to the ranch with him and treated some lechuguilla bucks.

It had been the experience of everybody in that country

that they always lost these sheep after they had gotten to the stage of "dry mouth." There was a polite kind of silence for a minute when somebody asked, "Are there any of 'em still alive?"

They all laughed, and I did too. Then Guy broke the news that his old Mexican ranch foreman had told him that every buck drank water and slobbered at the mouth and had a kidney action (which would usually dry it up) before we had had time to get back to town. Within a few days, all were drinking and were eating cottonseed meal and ground grain that was left in a trough of free choice. The fever had left them, their lips had peeled off, their heads were bright, and they were ready to be turned out of the hospital pen.

The atmosphere brightened and the conversation of those around the table and those joining us warmed up considerably and Pat Cooper very hurriedly and respectfully asked, "Doctor, what did you give them?" I cut him a little short, but laughed when I said: "That's a professional secret."

This was the first pleasant experience that I had had in weeks. My breakfast tasted better, and I left the hotel thinking that the poisonous plants of the Trans-Pecos Region of Texas were going to need far closer attention than I had imagined.

I had been practicing in Fort Stockton about two months and had moved from the motel to the Hubbs Apartment Building, and the drugstore and other people were taking my calls for me. As yet, I didn't have an office downtown.

The lechuguilla story spread fast, and the fact that no medication had ever been given a lechuguilla sheep or goat that seemed to have done him any good before caused the ranchers to pay me a little more mind.

Frank Hinde, who ranched about forty miles southeast of Fort Stockton, heard about the lechuguilla bucks and came into town, found me, and told me he had sixteen Angora goats in the corral that were as bad as lechuguilla goats could be and still be alive. He grinned and said, "If you can do 'em any good, I'd begin to believe you're a doctor, and it might be all right for you to stay in the country."

Frank was foaled in the West, grew up in sheep and cow country, and had cowboy'd all his younger life and graduated to a ranch when he was about middle age. He was a natural-born stockman and a very close observer. He could tell what a sheep or goat was thinking and was referred to by all the Mexicans in the country as "Pancho y medio" which in their language means "man and a half."

He was six feet eight inches tall, wore a high crown hat, high-heel and high-top boots that came to his knees and stuck his britches in his boot tops. If you could have seen him get out of a car or walk in a door, you would readily understand why they called him "man and a half." His generosity and humor were still on a larger scale.

I told him I could treat lechuguilla but my experience was very limited, that I could make no promises as to how the goats would do but I would be glad to come out and expose them to my professional ability.

I made this statement because it was dawning on me that very little was known about the poisonous plants of the Trans-Pecos Region, and I had hunted diligently through veterinary literature and no mention could be found about the plant or of its effects on any breed of domestic livestock that had eaten it. This was why I hedged a little instead of throwin' my chest out and actin' as if it was very simple to have sheep or goats that had eaten the plant.

Frank laughed and said, "They've been exposed to enough lechuguilla to kill 'em, so they couldn't be any worse off from your treatment."

I got to the ranch a little before midmorning the next day, and he was out at the goat corral with some Mexican ranch hands waiting for me. This was a bunch of fine Angora goats with lots of mohair on them. They were drawn and humped up with their faces blistered, their mouths sealed to, their eyes turning yellow, and were a pitiful sight. They would make very little effort to get away from a herder when he would go up to catch them.

I had had a few days to think about lechuguilla and to think about the therapeutic action of internal medicine. It's common knowledge that sheep and especially goats can eat and thrive on the leaves and bark of brush that cattle and horses cannot digest. The more I studied about it, the more I knew that it was not the impaction of dry fiber that was the killer; after all, there's an old saying that a goat can digest almost anything, even a board.

It is my professional opinion that the juice of the plant had astringent effects on the hair glands of the digestive tract that secreted the acids that would normally aid in the completed destruction of woody fibers. This was the reason I resorted to hypodermic injections and treatment by mouth with drugs that contained no purgative action but worked on the stimulation of the gland functions of the sheeps' and goats' bodies.

As we went about treating these goats, I explained my theory to Frank, and he said, "Doc, I never knew anybody to worry as much about a goat's belly before, so maybe you got something."

He went on to explain to me that the Sonora Experiment Station called it photosynthesis and said that the blistering of the face and swelling of the ears was the result of the absorption of the sun's rays. He hastened to explain that he had never believed a damn word of it, and if it proved out that I was wrong not to be hacked because at least I'd had a new thought about it.

During this conversation we had treated the sixteen goats, and Frank and his Mexicans were talking in Spanish about the few that might get well if they weren't treated. They pointed out three that had begun to peel off around the face and ears, which was an indication that they had passed the most dangerous stage and had a possibility of getting well.

We leaned against the fence and began to visit and talk about each one as we looked at them. I pulled out my watch and told Frank that all of them should begin to slobber at the mouth and lick their lips in about fifteen or twenty minutes. If my treatment was effective, these goats should drink water within an hour by reason of the fact that saliva had come back into their dried mouths and their lips had become moistened, which would bring feeling and taste back. Frank spoke up, "Any sheep or goat that will eat and drink will get well."

He turned and told his herders what I had said and one of them remarked that I would be "Mucho bueno, Doc-tor."

These goats had not drunk for the several days that they had been in this water lot, and about that time a weak little bitty yearling nanny walked up to the water trough and stuck her blistered mouth down into the cool water and licked her tongue out a few times and then drank so much that I stepped up and pushed her away from the trough. By noon every goat there had drunk and had begun to nibble at the alfalfa hay and the mixture of cottonseed meal and salt that was in the trough close to the water.

It was about dinnertime, so we went to the house, and Frank's wife, Ruth, had a big dinner for us. We had quite a visit, and Frank bragged on me and told me how glad he was that I was in the country.

He wasn't the timid sort, and it wasn't long before everybody knew how he felt about having a horse doctor in the Trans-Pecos ranch country. This message coming from him didn't hurt my future practice none.

As I drove back into town that afternoon, I was well pleased with my day's work. It was becoming more and more apparent to me that in order to practice veterinary medicine in an alkaline soil, semi-arid region, it was going to be necessary for me to buy some laboratory equipment and do a great deal of research so as to discover methods and formulas of treating livestock in this region that were almost unknown to veterinary science.

Both the drugstores were taking my calls, and I was still carrying my medical supplies and practicing out of the back of my car and cleaning up and sterilizing my instruments in my apartment. Each time I drove into town, I went to the drugstores to see if I had any calls. The word began to get around that there was a horse doctor in town, and I began to pick up some emergencies and light practice.

About two o'clock in the morning my phone rang and it was a very fastidious old woman who after some persuasion had caused me to do some surgery on her poodle dog. I had explained to her that the dog could not have any food for about twelve hours, but never in my practice did I ever say that any animal could not have a drink of water. Now this two o'clock call was to tell me that Charm was crying for a drink of water and would it be all right for her to have some. I hadn't been to bed very long and I wasn't too happy about Charm and her drink of water, but I thought better than to cuss this precise old social woman out and I just as well could have a little fun out of it.

In answer to her question, I asked, "Do you have any distilled water in the house?"

She said, "No, I don't have," just as though she kept it all the time and this was the first time that she was out.

I said, "Put some water in a pan and boil it for about thirty minutes, let it set until it's cool, and then it will be all right for Charm to drink all she wants of it."

Well, she was so grateful for my consideration of Charm's health, she said she would boil the water immediately. I figured that by the time she got the water to boil and sat up waitin' for it to cool, maybe she could go to sleep and wouldn't hear that dog cry and maybe I could get some sleep too.

By now my general practice had gotten to be rather steady, and all the early spring diseases and surgery were keeping me busy. It was time to begin doing the usual amount of spring surgery, mostly castrating young horses. As usual, ranchmen looked up the signs of the Zodiac before they ever came and asked me to work on their young horses. I never looked at the "signs" but I could always tell when they were supposed to be "right" because three or four different ranchers would want to make appointments to castrate their horses all about the same time.

I went to Guy Rochell's ranch one morning, and he had lots of good help to rope and tie as many as three horses down at a time. Guy carried my bucket of solution with my instruments in it from one horse to the next, and I carried my sulfa powder in a bottle in my hip pocket. Everything worked real fast and none of these horses had any unusual problems and from ten thirty till noon we caught, castrated, and turned loose twenty-seven head of horses.

It was good, sunny, dry weather and fresh green feed had grown enough for horses to fill up on it. I knew from the luck we had in the surgery and the medication I used that these horses would have to have gotten well without the slightest complication.

I was still new in the country and was hoping that my professional reputation was improving. I saw Guy Rochell standing in front of the Stockton Pharmacy talking with several other ranchers and thought that this would be a good time to get some complimentary remarks. As I walked up and shook hands, I said, "Mr. Rochell, how have the horses done? Did they swell any?"

Guy rared back and wrinkles formed over his nose, and in a complete expression of disgust and high tone of voice, he said, "Did they swell? Did they swell? They swelled the mares in another pasture."

Not too long after this, Bud Calhoun called and wanted me to come out to his place and castrate a two-year-old colt that he was very fond of. His place was just north of town in the irrigation valley that was watered by the natural flow of Comanche Springs. Bud made a business of repairing windmills, pulling sucker rods, and doing whatever was necessary to keep water flowing in the big pastures of the ranch country, and this farm where he lived was not his full-time work.

When I drove up, he had one man who worked for him and a neighbor there to help with the horses. As I began to get my instruments ready, Bud wanted to have a little talk with me. He was glad that I was in the country and all that kind of polite stuff, but directly, he cocked his head to one side and squinted his eyes and asked, "Did you ever cut a horse before?"

We talked on as I was gettin' ready for the operation, but I didn't give him any assurance that I knew what I was doing or that the horse would live or anything of the sort, and against his better judgment, we went ahead with the operation. We had plenty of rope, and the men helping were stout and didn't know a whole lot about tying down a horse but were willing. The colt was halter-broke and it didn't take long to get him on the ground.

I had him castrated in less time than it takes to put it on paper. When the men helping had all the rope off the horse, and I was about to get up off my knees and the colt made no effort to struggle or get up, I looked up over my shoulder at Bud. He looked awful pale and sick and you could tell he was sure enough worried about his pet horse. I cleared my throat and raised my voice right quick and asked, "Bud, what are you going to do with the hide?"

Just before I thought he might faint, I slapped the colt in the flank with my hat and squalled at him and kicked him real hard in the belly from the ground side, and he jumped up and ran off. Bud took a long breath and said, "Doc, you scared me. I don't know whether you're gonna do or not."

I had met Dow Puckett soon after I came to Fort Stockton, and he, like many others, had me do some dentistry and also remove tumors from backs and shoulders, and other light surgery on their horses. Most of this practice was an accumulation of neglect because there had never been a veterinary doctor living in Fort Stockton and they were not accustomed to being able to get some of these better livestock practices performed.

One Sunday afternoon in the summer, the cowboys were gathered over at the Sheriff's posse grounds for a calf roping. Lee Graves came into town with his horses, wife, and kids and had started to the roping. He had an awful bad jaw on him from a toothache, and it wouldn't get any better. He didn't want to miss that calf roping, so he stopped at the drugstore to see if he could get something to ease it.

Gallemore told him from the size of his jaw and looks

of his mouth that he ought to go to the dentist. He called Dr. Bailey at home but never got an answer and Gallemore said that he didn't have anything strong enough to do him any good that he could give without a doctor's prescription.

I had driven up in front of the drugstore and was gettin' out of my car when Lee came out the front door. He was holding that jaw, and I guess he was wondering how he was going to stand the pain and not miss the calf roping. Then he saw me. We were good friends and I had done some practice for the Hoover Ranch, where he was a partner with his Uncle Arthur.

He said, "Doc, I've got a toothache big enough for a horse, and I want to go to the calf ropin'. The way it's pumpin' and jumpin', it might affect my ropin' and you know that I need to get even with some of the boys from the last ropin'. Have you got anything that you could give me to kind of ease the pain?"

He explained that he had tried to get the dentist and that he guessed he was gone from home. Well, I didn't think Bailey was gone from home because I knew he didn't answer the phone on Sunday. I was interested in the performance at the calf roping because I was going to go watch. So I said, "Sure, Lee, I'll give you something 'cause I would consider it an emergency in the matter of tryin' to steady a man's hand who was going to a calf ropin'."

I reached in the back of my car and found the pills I wanted him to have and handed him two of them. I said, "Now, Lee, take one of these now, and wait about an hour, and if it hasn't quit hurtin', you can take the other one."

He turned and went into the drugstore to get a drink of water, and as he came back out, he said, "I sure thank you, Doc. If I win enough at the ropin', I'll cut you in."

Lee was riding a stud and like all cowboys at the roping, he was sitting at the back of the chutes on his horse waiting for his turn. This stud reached over and nipped a mare or two standing around him and before the other rider could stop her, she kicked that stud in the belly three or four times right quick.

About then they called Lee's name to rope and he broke out from behind the chutes and fitted the rope as pretty as you please so that they took up right behind the ears of that calf. As he stepped down on the ground, his leg went out from under him and he couldn't get up.

When the other cowboys carried him off the ground, I asked, "Lee, what's the matter?"

He said, "I took both of them pills at the same time and I was so numb that I didn't know that that mare broke my leg until I stepped off the stud to rope my calf."

ALKALI

During the time I had been in Fort Stockton, one of the other constant questions was, "What do you know about alkali?" This was the local name for livestock that were poisoned by eating goldenrod in the wintertime.

If veterinary science and research in a hundred years or more on the North American continent hadn't approached, much less solved, some of these many poisonous weeds, there was no use in me hedging or alibiing as to my lack of knowledge, and I began to answer, "I don't know, but I'll try to find out." Goldenrod poisoning was another one of these neglected unknowns.

I was sittin' in the drugstore one day when Dr. Moore

came in. He was a fine old family doctor who had come to the Trans-Pecos Region as a young man at the start of the First World War and was a bad tubercular, but the dry regions of the Southwest had caused him to be able to live a long, normal, useful life.

As we sat at the fountain, I brought up the subject of alkali. Dr. Moore related several experiences in his practice as an M.D. where people had become poisoned from drinking the milk from cows that were being pastured along the Pecos River and had access to goldenrod.

The earliest case history was that of two women who had died of poisoning near Grand Falls, Texas, and a kinsman had been accused of poisoning these old women for their wealth and was tried and convicted of the crime. In later years, Dr. Moore moved into the country and treated a family of five that had the same kind of symptoms and were poisoned. One of the family died before the milk of the cow was suspected as being the source of poisoning.

He told me of a number of cases where people had gotten alkali poisoning from drinking milk. He also said that for the last good many years, it was common knowledge that the poisoning was from grazing on goldenrod after the frost had caused it to be palatable to livestock.

I answered several calls that winter for alkalied cattle and horses. There were no symptoms in any of these cases of gastrointestinal disturbance. The weed was digestible and whatever the toxic substances were, they entered the blood stream. In the case of cows and mares that were giving milk, the grown animal would throw the toxic substance off in the milk and the calves and colts would die. Grown dry cows, steers, and bulls, when they had eaten goldenrod for several days, would appear normal until they were driven, moved, or hauled or in some manner exercised and excited, at which time they would develop an extreme

nervousness and would become stiff and go into severe rig-
gers and quiver and shake and lie down. Very few, if any,
would recover without careful treatment. There were some,
however, that were saved by keeping them quiet and carrying them feed and water; over a long period of time, it
seemed that they eliminated the toxic substance from their
systems, but, for the most part, the mortality rate was extremely high.

I did post-mortems on a number of cattle, some sheep,
and lots of horses during the winter and found very little
or no evidence in the organs of anything that would have
caused death. There were several big horse ranches along
the Pecos River that ran thousands of brood mares. They
generally expected to lose a lot of them in the winter and
had almost resigned themselves to this being one of the
hazards of ranching along the Pecos River.

Old Man Garner had a horse ranch on the Pecos River
running north from Girvin, and he ran his horses open
range. He rarely knew how many he had and wasn't too
concerned about losing horses because of goldenrod since
they were awfully cheap at the time.

I asked him about letting me know when one of his
mares died because I would like to do a post-mortem on her
as soon as possible.

"Doc," he said, "seems like you're tryin' to help the country, and me and them old mares ain't helpin' it much at
the price they'd bring. Why don't you come out whenever
you've got the time and get a saddle horse at the ranch
headquarters that's been on good feed and won't have no
goldenrod in him and ride up and down the river. Then,
anywhere you find a band of them mares, just jump 'em and
run 'em till one falls dead and do whatever you want to her
while she's still warm. Most any mare that you run and
cause to drop dead is gonna die before winter's over any-

way, so you just come back and hunt mares till you find out somethin'. I won't charge you nothin' and you don't charge me nothin'. Don't that seem like a fair proposition?"

Early in the mornings I would go out and saddle a good horse at the ranch headquarters. I'd take the small instruments I needed to do a post-mortem and put them in the pockets on my saddle that I could buckle down tight so there would be no danger of losing them. Then I tied the larger instruments to my saddle with the saddle strings.

All these range mares were wild and had been run at different times before they were corraled to cut their colts away from them to wean, and at the sight of a man on horseback, they would break and run. I would strike a hard run and holler a few times and they wouldn't go far before a mare's head would go down and her tail would fly up and she would roll over dead.

The first few times I ran these mares, I went through the normal post-mortem procedure without finding anything new. Early one cold February morning I jumped a bunch of range mares, and they didn't go far before one fell dead. I stepped off my horse. This time I had brought a small hatchet and I chopped through the ribcage and dissected the heart with several inches of the large arteries. I got about a teacup full of pure crystals out of these arteries and the cavity of the heart.

I had never opened any of the arteries before in this particular research, so I began to split open the larger blood vessels and discovered very fine crystalline substances deposited along the walls of the arteries. This explained the reason for sudden death without fever or any signs of disease. This substance from the juice of the goldenrod was digested, passed into the blood stream in liquid form, and then crystallized. At the increased heart rate from exercise or excitement, the crystals were jarred loose and accumulated in masses, which resulted in heart block.

It was after dark when I got back to my office. I had driven and worked hard all day, and I was awfully dirty and tired. I had my living quarters in the back of my office and was about to clean up when the phone rang.

The day before a very attractive young lady had brought a half-grown female collie for me to examine. All that was the matter with the dog was a severe infestation of intestinal parasites. The only treatment that could be prescribed at the time was a very harsh medication in liquid capsule form, and the patient had to be held off food for twelve to twenty-four hours before taking the pill. I had given this beautiful young thing some pills to give her dog the next night and that's who was callin'.

She said, "Doctor, I just cannot give this pill to Cynthia."

"Does she break them in her mouth and spit them out?" I asked.

She said, "No, I just can't give them to her."

Well, I was mad, tired, and short-tempered in those days and in my irritation said, "Why in the hell can't you? You're the biggest."

She said, "Well, I get down to her and almost get her mouth open when I see those big, soft, pleading eyes—and I just can't."

I asked, "Have you thought about takin' a towel and blindfoldin' the bitch and then givin' her the pill?" and hung up.

I had about finished cleaning up and was ready to do some lab work when someone knocked on the office door. I came out from the back through the office, and there was a smooth-faced, narrow-eyed, curly haired effeminate little man at the door. As he patted the sweat from his brow with a spotless handkerchief, he asked in a squeaky voice, "Are you Dr. Green?"

I said, "Yeah, what do you want?"

Straightening himself up and stammering he asked, "Did you call my wife a bitch?"

I thought a second, just as if I said things like that all the time, and said, "I don't know. Who is your wife?"

When he told me, I said, "No, I didn't."

He looked so relieved that he wasn't going to have to whip me, I said, "But as an afterthought . . ."

He said, "Never mind, sir, never mind," as he backed away from the door and left.

After this little interruption, I carefully washed the blood out of the crystals taken from the mare and by common laboratory tests identified barium sulfate and a number of other crystalline substances that wouldn't normally be classified as toxic. The medical problem here would be to neutralize these substances in the blood stream and cause them to become liquid by the use of therapeutic medicinal agents. By this process, in liquid form, these chemical properties could be eliminated by the kidneys and the victims could be saved.

I put out the word that I thought I could do something for alkalied cattle and horses, and I had a number of anxious stockmen hollerin' for help.

Harold Udaily at Grand Falls called me late one afternoon and said that he had heard that I had been saving some alkalied cattle and mentioned that he had a bunch of young registered bulls in a field east of Grand Falls and and several of them were down and the rest showed signs of alkali sickness.

It was bitter cold and the ground was frozen, and I told him that these cattle would have to be put in a pen where we could get hold of them. He explained to me that these registered bulls were all gentle and had been halter-broke when they were calves, and he thought we could treat them in the field. I agreed that would be better than having to move and exercise them.

I got to where the cattle were about dark, and Harold had brought George Bentley with him. The three of us slipped and stumbled around over the frozen ground and treated these bulls by car light. The treatment consisted of a muscular hypodermic injection and medicine by mouth. They were gentle and didn't exert themselves or cause us too much trouble.

George Bentley was a big, fat, good-natured fellow and his conversation probably offset the blizzard some, and his weight was real helpful as he stumbled around and fell on these cattle to hold them. He said he needed to take lessons 'cause he had some cattle that would sure go to gettin' sick as soon as they learned there was a new disease in the country.

There were fifteen of these bulls, and I left additional medicine to be given by mouth for the next few days. Harold was a good caretaker and nurse for these bulls and the entire bunch recovered.

The first formula that I compounded and the first hypodermic injections that I prescribed never had to be changed or improved upon since they were based on the actual analysis of the crystals discovered in the horse's heart. The recovery was governed by the gentleness and temperament of the patient more than anything else.

I spent that winter and several more wearin' out mud chains on my car in ice and bad weather and treated cattle and horses from as far south as Sheffield and answered calls along the Pecos River clear to Roswell, New Mexico. Before the winter was over, I almost wished I hadn't learned about the treatment for alkali. As winter turned into spring, the goldenrod soon played out, and I was mostly concerned with the usual run of general practice for the next two months.

One of the most prominent lawyers of Fort Stockton and a native son came in with a cocker spaniel pup whose tail he had attempted to dock but actually hadn't much more than cut off the tip of it. There had been enough time for the tail to scab over.

He was very apologetic and so remorseful about having cut the little pup's tail and having botched up the case instead of bringing me the pup in the first place. Well, I wasn't soliciting any small-animal practice and couldn't see that the pup looked any worse with a long tail than he would have with a short one. I was extremely busy and very much absorbed in some laboratory work I was doing, so in all seriousness, I explained to him that he had done exactly the right thing and that every two weeks he could repeat the operation until he got the tail as short as he wanted it, since taking it off a little at the time would keep it from hurting so much.

He thanked me graciously and offered to pay me, but I said I wouldn't think of charging him. I don't know how many days it took before it dawned on this legal mind just how stupid he was for believing my statement.

The desert makes few promises and holds many surprises and the summer flash floods brought on more weed problems, which made me realize that I would never be able to foretell the next rising poisonous plant. There had been some little flash floods up and down the draws but no real good grass-growing rains, and flocks were showing up with a good number of stiff sheep.

The Moss brothers, who were ranching west of Fort Stockton and northeast of Hovey, were in a rolling country not far from the foothills of the Davis Mountains and had gotten the earliest flash rains up and down the draws. John Moss was the first to come into the office talking about stiff sheep.

I went out to the ranch with him and looked at several hundred sheep in some stage of stiffness. John had moved them into a smaller pasture close to the headquarters. From his own observation he had determined that there were no new cases since he had moved them and he began to wonder what there was in the other pasture that had made them stiff.

I didn't offer to treat these first stiff sheep because I had already learned that there were a number of conditions that would cause sheep to stiffen, and in many instances, there would be no similarity between cases. Treatment for sheep that had stiffened in one locality would not necessarily be indicative for stiff sheep somewhere else.

I promised John that I would do some research in an effort to determine what caused the stiffness, and as soon as I knew something I would be back.

I saddled a horse the next morning and jumped him in the trailer behind my car and drove around over the country to the different locations where the first flash rains had fallen. I took my horse and rode out the draws that had flooded and looked for fresh growth, weeds, and brush.

It's rare to find a poison grass, so I gave special attention to any fresh tender weeds or new leaf growth or browse brush, hunting for vegetation that might be the source of the toxic substances that were causing sheep in open pastures to stiffen. The only weed I found in sufficient quantity for sheep to be getting a full diet of was a creeping red-stemmed, green-leafed milkweed that grows close to the ground and puts out with just a little moisture about this time of year. (There are other types of milkweed, but this is the one common to the Far Southwest desert regions.)

I drove back to town and unloaded my horse. I had a portable analytical laboratory kit built into a mahogany cabinet that fit in the back of my car, and late in the afternoon, I drove out into an overflowing draw thickly covered with this little creeper milkweed I had located earlier.

My instinct told me that if there was a toxic substance in milkweed, it would be most available after the chilling hours of the night, which would stop its growth temporarily, and the extract of its juices would be much simpler. Since it was early spring, after sundown the night would get uncomfortably cold. My practice was a good deal better than I needed it to be so far as getting any rest was concerned, and I curled up in the front seat of my car, pulled a Navaho blanket over me, and went to sleep.

When I waked up, the moon was high, the night was clear, and it had gotten cold enough to cause chemical reactions in the plantlife. I pulled some milkweed and began to run it through a portable squeezer that looked about like a clothes wringer. As I used a reagent on the sap from this weed, I extracted three different acids, each of which, to say the least, was mildly harmful, if at all. I went back to town and ran still more of this weed through my better laboratory equipment without any change or result.

The next night I went on the same trip hoping to gather fresh weed under range conditions, thinking maybe I had missed something in my observations the night before. As I worked another batch of this weed, about midnight I saw some sheep come in to water at a windmill, and there were a number of stiff sheep in the bunch.

I hadn't made any arrangements with the owner of this pasture or this flock of sheep, which was unnecessary since I was, for the most part, considered welcome in any of the ranch country. Even though many times I'm sure they thought I was off the beam, nearly everybody was tolerant of my mistakes, and I never bothered to ask permission to do anything I wanted to.

I took my .22 target and shot a stiff sheep in the moon-light, pulled him around in front of my car lights, cut him open, and quickly extracted some gastric juices that were secreted by the hair glands of the sheep's digestive system. I poured these gastric juices into a test tube and began add-ing the extract that I had made from the fresh milkweed and a few drops of a chemical reagent; suddenly I dis-covered that the toxic substances were being formed in the sheep's stomach from the combination of the milkweed juice and the secretion of the natural digestive acids of the sheep. By daylight I compounded in my laboratory a full treatment for sheep that were stiff from grazing creeper milkweed.

The next morning I took some of my new milkweed medicine to John Moss's ranch, and he and I treated about a hundred stiff mutton lambs. The sheep's recovery was quick and the treatment satisfactory, easy to administer by mouth and economical enough to use as often as needed. As soon as the rains came in other directions from town, there was a new crop of milkweed and I was ready with my milkweed prescription.

I came back to the office about noon and Seeino, who claimed to be half Gypsy and half Navajo Indian, was waitin' for me to look at a sick horse. Seeino was a drifter and an odd sort of a lone-wolf character who had moved into an old abandoned adobe house west of town near the railroad stock pens.

As we drove out to his place, Seeino told me, waving both hands Gypsy fashion, that this horse had a bad cut on his left shoulder. With the gestures of a Gypsy and the expression of an Indian, he said, "I use strong Indian-Gypsy medicine on my horse and it no work too good. I think maybe this horse raised by white man why medicine no work."

I followed his conversation as closely as I could as he went on to tell me, "I think maybe you have medicine to cure white man part of horse."

As we drove up to the corral, I saw what he meant by "STRONG" medicine: it was a fresh killed dog's head tied around the horse's neck with a wire.

He saw me looking at the dog's head instead of the sore shoulder and said, "I kill dog so dog's spirit take evil spirits out of horse's shoulder."

I studied his expression a few seconds and realized how much faith he had in that strong Indian-Gypsy medicine and said, "Seeino, you did exactly the right thing. It's just not a big enough dog to carry out all the bad spirits."

I told him the dog's head was causing the horse to be sad, and I unwired it and took it off as I explained that it would keep my medicine from working on the white man part of the horse.

When the horse got well Seeino offered to go partners with me. He explained that there was lots of Indian blood in Western horses and he'd get the Indian part of the horse well, and then if my medicine was strong enough to get the paleface part of the horse well, we'd never lose a horse.

SLEEPING SICKNESS

Charlie Baker, the sheriff of Pecos County, rushed into my office about nine o'clock one hot August morning and said, "Doc, there're four or five horses over at the Sheriff's posse barn fallin' around, and I know they've got the blind staggers. I've seen some of it when I farmed back East and they're got it if I ever saw it, and I'm afraid that the rest of the horses over there are goin' to start staggerin' soon. Ben K. is already weavin' a little when he walks. (Ben K. was a horse I had given him.) You know everybody that's got a horse over there thinks as much of them as they do of their families and you got to do somethin' fast."

"Charlie, it ain't likely that there is any blind staggers in this old desert country because it's generally caused by horses bein' fed moldy corn or some other feed that's in the process of sourin' after it's been wet."

"Well, I'll swear it looks just like blind staggers."

As I stepped into my car, I said, "I'll follow you to the posse barn."

News had spread fast and there were several of the fellows who had horses in the posse barn already there when I drove up. They were leading and holding four horses out in the corral in front of the barn that were having a hard time being still or walking straight. At a glance I knew that we had a fresh outbreak of sleeping sickness, and I explained to everybody that it might be easier to cure and stop the spread of it than blind staggers because there were serum injections for the treatment of sleeping sickness and vaccines to stop it from spreading.

Encephalomyelitis is a disease of horses that is spread by blood-sucking insects that transmit the disease from one horse to another; this explains why it is a late-summer and fall disease, for it is then that the transporting hosts are most prevalent. It is commonly referred to among horsemen as "sleeping sickness."

When a horse has been bitten by an insect carrying the virus, he will slowly develop the virus in his blood stream; it takes about five or six days. When the disease becomes apparent, the first symptoms are nervousness and a difficulty with vision, and a gentle horse will have trouble recognizing the person who has been handling him.

After this first stage, the horse becomes unsteady on his feet and wobbles and staggers and stands with his head lowered toward the ground, and as he becomes worse, he will find a fence or tree or some other solid object to push against with his breast or shoulder to steady himself. This is getting into the last stages.

The next step in the disease is that the horse falls to the ground and is unable to regain his equilibrium. After this happens, no matter how much treatment and care a horse may get, should he recover he will never be the same because the damage to his central nervous system will leave him more or less stupid and without good coordination, even though he may appear to be normal.

There had been a few cases of sleeping sickness in the area in the late summer every year. This had been a rainy summer, so to speak, for a desert region and flies and mosquitoes were plentiful. A good many of my regular clients had me vaccinate their horses for sleeping sickness early enough to prevent the disease. However, these horses would amount to a very small percentage of the horse population in the Trans-Pecos, Edwards Plateau, and Davis Mountains Region. These areas had gotten to be my over-all territory.

In late August I was called for a few cases of sleeping sickness that were widely scattered over my practicing territory. By the first week in September there was a full-scale epidemic of sleeping sickness raging among the horse population. I was ordering vaccine for the inoculations and anti-serum for the treatment in such high amounts that the laboratories were beginning to short my orders but were sending all they could, which in many instances wasn't enough. I began phoning drugstores and other practitioners in regions where there had not been an outbreak and buying up all the available stock I could find while the laboratories hurried in their efforts to produce fresh supplies.

The harder and the faster I worked, it seemed the more the epidemic got out of hand. There were thousands of stock horses, brood mares, yearlings, two's, and so forth that weren't being vaccinated and were a constant source of new infestation to the gentle horses that were in the working remuda on the various ranches. It seemed that horses being kept on feed around ranch headquarters or in town so that they would be available for immediate and everyday use were getting sick in greater numbers than range horses. This was true because of the additional population of flies and mosquitoes around barns, corrals, watering places, and the like.

The vaccination was a 1-cc. live-virus injection administered between the layers of the skin (interdermal). Because of the slow absorption of this skin shot it took at least nine days to begin to furnish some immunity, and it was necessary to vaccinate the horse with a second shot seven days after the first one. Within three weeks I had vaccinated about three thousand horses and had about two hundred and fifty active cases of sleeping sickness under treatment.

The usual treatment for a horse already stricken with the disease was to inject into the juglar vein 250-cc.'s of anti-serum. In addition to this I always gave some heart stimulant, the purpose of which was to keep the horse on his feet. Often when an owner would describe a horse's condition to me over the phone and I knew that it would be a few hours before I could possibly get to him, I would instruct that a quart of strong black coffee to be given by mouth every two hours until I got there. This was another way to keep a horse awake and on his feet. Many of those good telephone operators who served the ranch country of the Far Southwest mercifully would sometimes be guilty of listening in and asking somebody that couldn't get in touch with me how sick their horse was and several learned to tell them to drench their horses with a quart of strong black coffee until they could reach me.

This was a big ranch country and I was driving unbelievable distances, making very few stops other than to get gas and supplies. These were the war years and the local ration officer caught up with me about noon one day and told me there was a man from Washington, D.C., in his office who came to check my gas mileage and would ride along with me for a few days in my practice. I had had very little sleep, ate when I could get to it, and was drawn down pretty hard and mean, so I said, "Brush the brain-washed civil service idiot out on the curb and I'll suck him up directly."

I whipped by the courthouse and this very nice precise gentleman of about thirty-five was standing on the curb in front of the courthouse when I stopped. As I got out of the car, he asked, "Are you Dr. Green?"

I told him, "Yeah," and he introduced himself by saying that he was the civil service idiot who I was supposed to suck up. He had been on an extension line when Mr. Johnson, the chairman of our local board, was talking to me.

I had started to Marathon sixty miles south on a graded road. As we pulled out of town he took out a pencil and pad and went to figurin' and explainin' to me at the suggested word rate that at the speed of 45 mph in a ten-hour day with time out for meals and stops, it was hardly possible for one driver to drive one car more than three hun-

dred miles. The record showed that I was consistently getting over five hundred miles of gas-ration stamps a day,
figured at the rate of fifteen miles per gallon.

At the time he was makin' me this speech, I was driving
at 85 mph. I hadn't driven less than eighteen to twenty-
four hours a day in over two weeks and wasn't payin' a
hell of a lot of attention to what he was sayin'. However,
I had looked him over pretty good as was my habit with
livestock, women, and civil service employees.

He had the ruddy complexion of a freshly peeled banana
and his eyes were sort of marble-like of an indeterminate
color, and when you glanced at him through those thick
horn-rim glasses, you could almost see a column of figures
crossing the stare he wore. His nose and chin and the rest
of his face were narrow and sharp and you could have
jabbed both his eyes out with a hairpin without spreadin' it.
His hairline hovered down close to his eyebrows, and the
back of his head ran down his neck. After lookin' at him
carefully, I would say that he had a very typical kind of a
government head, and he had adorned it with a small
crown, narrow-brimmed brown hat that you could barely
get thumb-hold on.

We drove up to the Hess Ranch and the foreman by the
name of Hill waved me to come on down to the barn. I got
out and started talking with him and walked into the corral where the sick horses were and also those that he had to
vaccinate. He glanced over the fence and saw my passenger
sittin' in the car with the door open and asked, "What's
that?"

I told him who this passenger was and why he was along
and that he was a native of Maryland. Hill walked back to
the car with me, and on the way he said he wanted to take
a closer look at this gov'ment man.

I introduced Mr. Hill to Mr. Stratsford. Hill stuck his

long, strong callused hand out, and as he shook hands, you could tell he was tryin' to break every bone in that pencil-muscled hand as he said, "Hello, 'Fed.' I'm glad the gov'-ment has begun to pay old Doc some mind."

We circled by Alpine from Marathon and out to some ranches and back down the public highway between Alpine and Fort Stockton to the Hoovey Draw country. By now it was dark and I was still going from ranch to ranch treating horses that were already stricken with sleeping sickness. Along about five o'clock in the afternoon I noticed that he had put his little scratch pad and pen in his pocket.

We came out on the Balmorhea–Fort Stockton highway and turned toward town, a distance of about thirty miles. When I let him out about eleven o'clock that night at the Springhurst Hotel, I had crisscrossed and driven about three hundred miles since I picked him up. He had insisted that I not make any calls without him so I told him to eat something, get some rest, and I would pick him up just as soon as I had to make a call.

I had my living quarters in the back of my office, so I went in and started to go to bed when the phone rang. It was another case at Imperial, which was forty miles north of town, and I told them I would be right out. The telephone operators voluntarily kept tickets on my incoming calls and promised people who were phoning me that they would give me the message when they found me or when I called in.

I pulled up in front of the hotel and told Benny Walker, the night porter, to get my man for me. He had barely had time to take a bath, so he put on his clothes and came back down lookin' rather shocked, worn, and surprised that I would answer another call so soon.

The morning before he had taken a reading of my speedometer and had forgotten to look at it again when we got in that night. As we started off he looked at the speed-ometer and you could see some surprise come over his Maryland-bred, Washington-trained countenance.

I had some twenty-five or thirty horses to treat and vac-cinate at Imperial between then and daylight. The telephone operator from Fort Stockton caught me at the country café in Imperial and so I made some more calls north and west to Grand Falls and Monahans. Then we whipped back by Crane and McCamey and were back in Fort Stockton about three o'clock that afternoon. This was another three hun-dred plus miles, which made a total of more than six hundred miles in about twenty-four hours which was the distance between the places where I worked.

Between nine and ten o'clock that night I had a call from Jim Nance, the sheriff at Sanderson, about a horse of his that was at Charlie Gregory's ranch ten miles west of San-derson. I went by the hotel and picked up the "Fed" and we started sixty miles south to Sanderson. Jim's horse was sick but was in the early stages and I almost knew that the one treatment would be all that he would need, but by flashlight and lantern we vaccinated Charlie's best brood mares and saddle horses.

In the meantime, Frank Warren had put in a call from the Circle Dot Ranch in the Big Canyon that had been re-layed to me by Jim Vance, so we went from Sanderson to the Circle Dot. Frank didn't have his horses ready and told me when I could catch the time that I could come, call him in a day or so, since he didn't actually have a sick horse and this was just a vaccination call.

I went from the Circle Dot to Sheffield, about another seventy miles, and vaccinated horses there early the next morning and then we ate a bite of breakfast at one of the country cafés. I had had calls catch up with me to go to Iraan, where I vaccinated a bunch of horses and treated for Mr. Lee a horse that was already in secondary stages, which meant that I would have to double-check and stop by there every chance I got the next few days and nights.

Val Gobert went with us around Iraan to show us where all the different horses were that people had ready for me to vaccinate and he opened gates and entertained Mr. Fed for two or three hours. By now I had calls back to Sanderson.

We drove in under the long driveway at McKnight's Garage at Sanderson. It was a big old garage with a lot of loafers' benches just under the shade of the driveway and a big café at the end of the building. We got out of the car, so it could be serviced while we went in to eat. There were several loafers on the old car seats that were set out for that purpose. They all got up to shake hands and ask about people over the country. I had a pretty good audience, so I turned to my passenger and said, "Boys, I want you to meet Uncle Sam."

They all shook hands kind of polite as they looked him over, and as Monte Cordor shook hands with him, he said, "Doc's kind of a smart aleck. What's your real name?"

He put the Maryland brogue to it and told him the name was Stratsford. Between the length of the name and his foreign accent, another cowboy spoke up and said, "Monte, don't you wished you hadn't asked?"

I explained to them his mission in the Far Southwest and the reason he was with me, and as we turned to walk into the café, somebody said in a loud voice, "Why don't you let him drive some. We need to get our money's worth out of that kind of gov'ment help."

They served good Western grub and it was about middle of the afternoon, and Uncle Sam's appetite improved to the point where he ate as much as I did.

On the way back to Fort Stockton we went by Frank

Hinde's and I introduced Frank to Uncle Sam. Frank took an aerial view of him from his six feet eight inches, and he wore a high-crown broad-brimmed hat that made him look even taller. He shook hands with him and was so polite and nice that you could tell he didn't really mean it. It was gettin' real late in the afternoon, so Uncle Sam stayed in the car.

As Frank and I walked to the corral, Frank said, "What's the matter with that damn feller's head?"

I said, "I haven't diagnosed it yet."

"Well, it looks like he should cover it up with a bigger hat so he wouldn't look so bad."

That was a good enough opening for me to cut an old friend, so I said, "That explains why you wear such a damn big hat."

As we were driving into town that night, Uncle Sam began to break down. He had seen more country, more horses, and more rough roads and a different breed of people than he had ever imagined existed. He had seen us vaccinate wild horses in chutes or rope and choke them down and vaccinate them in a matter of a split second before they could get off the ground, and all in all he was impressed beyond words with his experiences and my professional talent combined with my cowboy and ranch background.

As we drove down the road between stops, I had explained to him some of the finer points that made it possible to work with a horse affected by sleeping sickness, even one that was staggering, and told him that you might slap a horse on the side where you were standing or raise your voice some and holler in his ear but never push against him because he would think that he had found something to lean against and you couldn't possibly hold him up and he would very likely fall on you. As I walked with a horse trying to put a needle in his jugular vein, I would put my free hand on the other side of his neck and pull toward me, which would cause him to stagger away from me, making it safer to give him an injection.

Whether Uncle Sam knew it or not, he was seein' cowboy'n' and horse handlin' at its best by lifetime experts.

As we got nearer town, he said that if he wrote his report and tried to explain the distances between calls and the vast amount of country I was covering, and describe the friendly, informality of the people, from his experience, Washington would send out another "brain-washed civil service idiot" to see if his report was true. He readily confessed that he never would have believed any part of what he had seen if it had just been told to him or written up in a report. For ten miles he was almost a human being and actually showed some kind of admiration for me, my clients, and the great Far Southwest.

I let Mr. Civil Service Expert out at the hotel and told him I would call him when I had to leave town again. It was about four o'clock in the afternoon and I lay down to take a nap and slept until almost dark. This was the first time in over a week I had been on a bed. I would catch a nap here and yonder in my car while I would be waiting for an owner to get his horses in the corral or during some other short delay.

My phone rang a little after dark and I had several calls stacked up in a matter of a few minutes. I loaded the refrigerated vaccine boxes in the back of my car and picked up other fresh supplies.

I pulled up in front of the hotel and told Benny to get my man. He said, "Doc, what have you done done to that feller! He took a bath and took a plane, an' he acted plum fitified about gettin' a taxi to take 'im to the airport and get away from hea'. He looked like he needed some res'."

Every horse owner had vaccinated every active case and

the neighbors who had pet horses and using horses had all vaccinated too, but it seemed that there would be no end to the epidemic; and now after three weeks, the disease was still spreading and I hadn't turned down a call and had lost very few cases. Any horse being treated for a disease that is accompanied by high fever and severe dehydration might get over the disease but die from the exhaustion and malnutrition that had occurred during the time of the most severe part of the sickness. Almost any sick animal with a raging fever will have the presence of mind or enough instinct to drink, but few if any will eat feed. All the cases that I had that were not beyond the secondary stage and hadn't gotten down, I fed by means of stomach tube and pump. I carried hundred-pound sacks of oatmeal and gallon jugs of molasses in the back of my car and as soon as a horse showed response to treatment, I would mix up in a tub a gruel of oatmeal, syrup, and sufficient water to make the mixture thin enough to go through a stomach pump. With the nursing and care of the owners, we rarely lost a horse that was still standing when I got to him for the first time.

Dick Arnold, a transplanted Vermonter who had come to the Far Southwest as a very young man and had aged out in the business, was still looked on by many of his neighbors as misplaced rather than transplanted. Dick had lots of horses and I was always doing some practice for him. He called early in the morning to tell me that he had three sick hosses and for me to come pa'pared to treat and vaccinate all his hosses.

Tires were very scarce, and although I had three permits from the ration board in my pocket to buy tires, there were no tires available; I had borrowed the spare tire from three different people's cars. I owned one tire that was on the ground, hopin' every day that some of the filling stations in town would be lucky enough to get a shipment of what we called war tires, which were mostly synthetic rubber.

Dick's ranch was between fifty and sixty miles south and I got to within about a mile of the ranch house when I blew out a tire. It was a country road with very little traffic, and after I blared my horn and hollered a few times, Dick drove up the road in a new Packard to see about me.

We loaded in his car all the medicine and vaccine that I would need to treat his hosses, and I decided that I would worry about the tire when I got through with the stock. During this period everybody tried to help those of us who needed to travel in order to be of service to the community, and I knew that Dick would have his men help me repair that tire one way or another.

He did have three very sick horses that we treated first and then vaccinated one hundred and four head. It was noon and Dick had a good housekeeper and cook who called from the back porch that dinner was ready. By now I had noticed that both of Dick's pickup trucks had brand-new tires on them, and as we went into the screen porch, layin' over in one corner were two more new tires, but I could see at a glance that they were truck tires and wouldn't fit my car. The thought ran through my mind that Dick had some better source of gettin' tires, black market or otherwise, than I did.

We got in place, as was the custom of the country, and went by the kitchen stove and helped ourselves to the barbecue, beans, and potatoes that were in Dutch ovens on the top of the stove. After I had eaten a big dinner in a hurry, I stepped up from the table, reached for my hat, and said, "Dick, I've got to go."

He said, "Don't hurry me. I'll get my hat."

While he was comin' off the porch, I stepped in that big

new Packard about two hundred feet away, started the motor, and slammed the door and as I waved at Dick, I hollered to him, "Bring my car to town after you get new tires on it."

I looked back in the mirror and saw him stompin' the ground and whippin' himself with his hat: I had thought about askin' him for a pickup, for he would have gladly loaned me one, but then he wouldn't have been worried about gettin' me new tires for my car. Since he always owed me a good deal more than a set of tires would cost, I knew that he would make the necessary arrangements, fair or foul, to get that new Packard back as soon as possible.

On the third morning at about daylight he drove up in front of the office in my car, which had four new tires on the ground and a spare in the turtle. We both had a big laugh and went up to the hotel and had breakfast together and traded automobile keys and drove on.

My day's work started by heading east to the Baker-White Ranch Company, where Pete TenyCke was foreman. He didn't have a sick horse, but he had a bunch of good horses that he wanted vaccinated.

Next I had a lot of work to do at the Elrod Ranch at Sheffield and went on across the Pecos River to Vic Montgomery's, where I vaccinated his horses and treated a sick stud, but not for sleeping sickness: he had a heart condition. I went on to Ozona and treated several horses in town in people's backlots.

By now it was night and I was way past due up north of Ozona around Rankin and Crane. I drove into Crane that night and gave some further treatment to horses that I had treated a few days before. I went on into Midland, where there was a Chrysler garage that had an all-night service department.

Midland was one hundred and ten miles north of Fort

Stockton and sort of the north edge of my territory. I got over there rather often and the night crew always serviced my car while I went across the block to the Scarborough Hotel and got some sleep; because I was away from home the chances were good that I wouldn't be bothered. The next morning I would start out in a car that had been well serviced while I slept.

I was never a very good businessman and always a poor bookkeeper and this Chrysler car was sort of a dirty sand color, so I used the outside of the cab for bookkeeping purposes. When I made a call, either before I left or the next time I stopped I would take my pencil and write the amount of the call somewhere on the outside of the car and put an initial of some kind on it so I would know whose it was and then draw a circle around it. This was all the bookkeeping system I needed since I rarely sent out bills. When a rancher would see me in town and say that he had sold something, such as lambs, wool, or cattle, and wanted to pay me, we would walk out to my car and I would look around on it for his bill. During the time we were doing this, we would be discussin' what all we did to the livestock the time that I made his call.

I cared very little about a car; it was just a means of transportation. And although I had one serviced, I never had one washed. This particular night after I had gone, the service crew were talkin' about all the business I gave them and the fact that I never got a wash job, and to show their appreciation for me coming by, after they got through greasin' and packin' the wheels, they just gave me a great big wash job, free—and I lost my books!

People who have never lived horseback and are not familiar with the big pastures in rough country would not understand the feeling that is developed among all members of a ranch family for certain individual horses. During this epidemic I rarely, if ever, heard discussed the value in dollars of a horse that was sick. The conversation about an older horse would concern the "good he had done" in helping establish a ranch or in helping raise the kids. In talking about one of the younger horses that were hard from constant use, the stories would be about the bad spots he had carried his rider through in working stock and how much endurance he had in rough country.

One night I was treating a horse that was sick and staggering bad but had not been down on the ground. As I walked and staggered with him, trying to get a needle in his jugular vein, the old cowboy leadin' him and holdin' his head and talkin' to him said, "Doc, I've dropped my rope into lots of wars on this old friend and we always won 'em, and we sure need to save him if we can." This meant that he caught lots of fightin' cattle and horses and brought them in and this horse was worth saving.

It was a common thing for a rider to leave the headquarters early in the morning and if in the late afternoon, he hadn't gotten back, when word got out, the first conversation would be about the horse he was ridin'. If his wife or somebody spoke up and said he was on a certain old horse that was known to be trustworthy, there would be a feeling of reassurance that he just had had some trouble but would be in after a while.

In the event a rider was past due to come in and someone remarked that he was ridin' a "green" horse (an inexperienced animal) or a horse that had a lot of endurance and was used for hard rides but was known not to be dependable in a tight, then whoever was around and whoever could be called easily would start lookin' for the rider, who might be crippled or killed. Horses that had no affection for people

and were undependable would rarely come back to a headquarters and would usually be found grazin' or at a water
hole.

When I was doctor'n' a horse, the story would come up
about what he had done and who he had saved and they'd
say, "Save him if you can!" Nobody in the ranch country
ever insulted a good horse by talking about what it would
cost to replace him and the telephone operators whose help
was indispensable in this particular epidemic were mostly
all girls and women with ranch background or were
married to a cowboy and the general thought in treating
horses was never about money but instead was to save the
horse for the good he had done or for what he meant to
somebody.

One night I was way below Sanderson on the Rio Grande
River treating some horses and the ranch wife came to the
corral and said, "We just talked to the telephone operators
and they have gotten together and figured out that you
haven't been to bed in about nine days. They told me to
tell you that so far as they know, your calls are sort of
caught up, and I should put you to bed."

This kind of concern was very touching, but I had more
work lined up than they knew about, so I thanked the good
woman and kept on doctorin' horses. When I left the ranch
and pulled out into the highway, I noticed several hot bis-
cuits stuffed with venison steak layin' in the seat of my car.
During these several weeks, the ranchwomen in the country
kept me fed by havin' food ready at the most ungodly hours
or by puttin' it in the car so I could eat on the way.

By the end of the fifth week the epidemic slowed up and
by then I had vaccinated (two injections) over four thousand horses and had treated three hundred and seventy-five
active cases and had driven over thirteen thousand miles.
Outside of the cavalry, there have never been this many

horses vaccinated or treated during the same length of time and over as wide a territory. This siege could not have been brought under control without the help of everyone who was interested in the horses of the great Southwest. The highly mechanized, direct-dialing telephone systems now in existence could have never performed the service to the ranch people and to me that those switchboard operators had, voluntarily and without any thought of gain or reward. Filling-station operators, café waitresses, druggists, and some few others all helped by taking and relaying messages.

YELLOWWEED
TERRITORY

From the day that I first met Con Cunningham on the street he confronted me daily with questions about yellowweed and insisted that I try to learn something about the treatment of sheep affected by it. After the streak of good luck I had had with lechuguilla, more ranchers became insistent that I "try my hand" on yellowweed.

I had become considerably more interested in yellowweed than the ranchers realized, but I'd begun to hedge and not ask as many open questions and had also begun to ponder what the financial return would be if by research I could develop a satisfactory antidote or treatment for sheep grazing on yellowweed. There were no figures available and no estimates that were accurate as to how many thousands of acres of yellowweed were in the Trans-Pecos Region and no fairly accurate guess as to how many sheep were being partially grazed on yellowweed.

Ernie Hamilton represented a livestock loan company, and was an old sheepman who covered most of West Texas in his job. He told me he thought that some quantity of yellowweed was found in as many as ten counties in West Texas and southeastern New Mexico. I had become well acquainted with the growth characteristics and appearance of the weed and decided that I would make my own personal survey to try to determine the territory that it covered.

The more I studied the weed the more I realized that it restricted itself to certain types of soil and terrain. In a good pasture next to a yellowweed growth, the soil and drainage might be such that the weed would not spread into it. It was rather inexplicable why it thrived on what was not necessarily the best soil.

I drove north from Fort Stockton and found an abundance of yellowweed nearly everywhere along the highway running from Fort Stockton to Pecos. But in a good part of this country there was barbed wire fence for cattle and no net wire fences for sheep, which meant that the weed was not a problem in that part of the country. However, I found yellowweed as far north as Lovington, New Mexico, and scattered amounts of it almost everywhere in southern New Mexico, but some of the sheep in this particular country were under herd and were kept from the yellowweed ridges.

West of Fort Stockton and all of Pecos County was yellowweed country. The Davis Mountains regions didn't furnish any yellowweed of importance, but I found several hundred sections of scattered weed in Culberson County and even in parts of Hudspeth County. To the south of Fort Stockton, in the southern part of Pecos County there was very little yellowweed and hardly any in Terrell and Brewster counties. There was lots of yellowweed east and slightly north of Fort Stockton all the way to McCamey and plenty in Upton and Crane counties, but most of that land was not being pastured with sheep.

My final analysis showed that Fort Stockton and Pecos County was for sure the capital of the yellowweed range in the West. Another peculiar finding was that very little yellowweed grew east of the Pecos River in the Edwards Plateau. In later years I transplanted some yellowweed that failed to make seed in that part of the country. With this information at hand and knowing that there were as many as a hundred thousand sheep subjected to the possibility of yellowweed poisoning, I decided to begin research on the weed.

One morning I met Dow Puckett in front of the hotel and told him that I had some ideas that I would like to experiment with on some sheep. I would put them in a small pen and feed them yellowweed, keeping them off any other feed.

Dow said, "I think that's fine, Doctor. I've got a number of sheep that will die from yellowweed before the winter's over anyway, so I'll bring you some of them. How many do you want at a time?"

I thought for a minute and said, "Until I find out how much weed they will eat per day, I think I would like to have four to put in the first pen; that will make percentages easier to figure both in my formulas and in the days of weed and days of death."

Dow laughed and said, "I don't think you'll learn much from four dead sheep, and I'll be willing to furnish you more as you need them."

The next day he brought the sheep in a pickup. The old Sheriff's posse barn was across Comanche Creek from town. I built panel pens on the outside of the barn, where we kept these yellowweed sheep.

The next day Doug Adams saw me at Dee Walker's filling station and said, "Doc, I heard that you and some sheep are eating yellowweed."

I said, "That's right and from what I've begun to learn from yellowweed, I may get sicker on it than they will before this is over."

He laughed and said, "I've been on and off it all my life, and I can promise you that it won't improve your health or your pocketbook."

As I started to leave, he said, "If you kill off all of Dow's sheep, I think I've got some to spare that the weed wouldn't be foreign to."

Not long after that, Ernie Hamilton was making his rounds for the loan company. These sheep had been on weed for several days and one was already showing signs of sickness and was beginning to vomit some weed. Ernie looked them over, gave me some encouragin' speech and said, "As much as feed bills and death loss have cost the loan company, I'll tell some of my customers that we'll give 'em credit if they give you some sheep."

I said, "Ernie, it may make it awful hard for your customers to keep up their head count if this research lasts as long as some think it will."

I pulled yellowweed every day up and down the bar ditches and in various pastures where it was lush and tender and I fed these sheep an exclusive diet of fresh yellowweed.

My practice had become real good and when I was too busy to pull yellowweed, Dow Puckett, Harrison Dyke, or somebody else would and feed these experimental sheep. Everyone was interested in what I was doing and it was the subject of conversation whenever I stopped for even a minute around the drugstore or filling station.

None of the first several medications that I administered to these sheep, whether by injection or dry powder mixed in feed or liquid medicine given by mouth, seemed to be of any particular value, and each bunch of experimental sheep would show yellowweed sickness from the fifth to the seventh day of the test. Without exception, by the eleventh day in a number of tests the first sheep would die.

Many times when I would be discussing yellowweed there would be talk about whether certain parts of the plant might be more poisonous than others. In one flock of experimental sheep I noticed that a big ewe lamb was especially fond of the blooms and would eat all of them off the fresh weed before she ate any of the stalk or leaves. An old Navajo sheep that I had fed several different ways preferred the dry stalk of last year's growth. Another ewe lamb would nibble the fresh leaves off the stalk and refuse to eat the tougher parts of the plant. I fed these three sheep separate a full diet of their choice part of the weed, and they all developed sickness within a few hours of each other. During this same period of time, I had fed the fresh pulled roots to rabbits and they developed the sickness at the same time that other rabbits got sick on the whole weed, so there was no part of the weed that did not contain the toxic substance and in equal proportions to the rest of the weed.

With one exception, by the twenty-first day, they were all dead. However, regardless of their state of sickness, they never ceased to eat fresh pulled yellowweed and would do so eagerly. In several instances they would prefer fresh yellowweed to alfalfa hay when both were put in the feeder at the same time.

The first of the formulas that I used were products of modern medicine and in many instances were hypodermic injections known to have desirable effects in the treatment of some other toxic conditions. All of these were completely worthless and caused me to turn my attention to some of the very old drugs of botanical origin that I had either used or knew to have been used for large livestock that were sick in other desert regions of the world.

I didn't have a lot of faith in this old witch medicine, but I had begun to think that maybe yellowweed was a witch too. Some of my treatments were in a sense farfetched. I ordered old botanical drugs that were in many instances obsolete, and sometimes the supplies I received showed signs of having been stored for a long time.

I gave some sheep a brown powder that was a combination of things that I had seen camel drivers use for what they called wet sickness in camels. I had also seen them give this same powder to their milking sheep—some Arabs have a breed of sheep that they keep instead of goats.

I also used medical preparations that I had found in the writings of early-day sheepmen in Australia, but these proved to be of no help. One time I even fed the sheep some skunk cabbage and seaweed from an old "Dr. Le-Gears's" prescription. They improved remarkably for several days and showed an increasing appetite and a thriftier, more alert appearance but that soon vanished and they went the way of all yellowweed sheep. I determined later that they showed improvement for a few days because they were iodine-deficient and the seaweed had been of benefit to them.

After I tried twenty formulas that didn't work, I began to take a much more serious look at the yellowweed problem. I moved into an office and installed a good practical laboratory and began doing extensive laboratory analyses of the internal organs of each sheep that died.

I was grinding yellowweed every day in a specially built grinding mill. The containers were made of porcelain, and porcelain balls of various sizes were placed in the porcelain barrel and set on a mill that turned the barrel over, and the falling of the balls ground the yellowweed to a pulp so that the juice could be extracted and the fiber analyzed microscopically. Porcelain equipment was used so as to prevent any chemical reaction from occurring in the grinding of the weed since the porcelain was neutral and no metal surfaces were involved.

Ranchers and town people alike were constantly encouraging me to work on this yellowweed project because it was of such major economic importance to this sheep-ranching country. Summer caused the weed to mature and become tough and other vegetation grew and so my yellowweed research had to be postponed until the following winter, but I was never allowed to forget the fact that I had started the project.

One day in the drugstore, I said something sharp and unpleasant to Gallemore, and Concho Cunningham had turned up his hearing aid and quickly turned to Gallemore and said, "Don't pay any attention to him. You remember he was on yellowweed all winter."

BANDITOS

Soon after I settled in Fort Stockton, Pete Williams from McCamey, forty-five miles away, visited me and told me of all the opportunities there were at McCamey for a veterinary doctor. He had some good horses that needed various routine things done for them, and there was some racehorse interest in and around the town, with a lot of other general practice. He and I agreed that I would come to McCamey every Monday morning until such a time as they didn't need me this often.

Pete Williams, a retired oilfield contractor, lived on the east side of McCamey. He was a very accommodating fellow and was known and liked by everybody and made a real good contact for me at McCamey for many years. He and Doc Halimacek at the drugstore in McCamey would write down all the calls that people had left for me that were not of an emergency nature. Then Pete would go along to show me where people lived and open gates and help with the livestock and visit with his neighbors. At the end of the day's work, anybody that had left word for me to vaccinate a dog or work a horse's teeth or anything else that hadn't been at home when we got there, Pete would give me his personal check for all that hadn't paid me and then do his own collecting. This was a good arrangement in that I didn't charge full mileage on one call because I would get a big enough day's work that I could divide a small amount of mileage be-

tween the calls of the day and nobody was hurt by the charges.

A year or two later a racetrack was built at McCamey by a group of public-minded citizens. I took a little stock in the track and racing was held every Saturday and Sunday. Dr. Cooper, an M.D. in McCamey, had a little bay mare named Golden Slippers. She was a sure 'nuff racehorse and outran 'most every horse that was brought in from other places for matched races.

Golden Slippers developed a serious kidney block one night. I was out on other calls, and it was about three o'clock in the morning when I got the word to come to McCamey.

In the meantime some of the stable hands drenched the mare by using a long-necked bottle and pouring the drench down through her nose. This could be done by a skilled person, but a much safer way would be to use a tube and pass it through the passage in the nose to the throat. I always gave liquid medicine as drench by mouth.

The stable hands made the fatal mistake of pouring sweet spirits of nider into Golden Slippers's lungs. I worked with her the rest of the night, knowing that there was no real hope of saving her. However, I gave her sedatives, trying to make her dying as painless as possible, and she died about daylight.

By this time there were several other horsemen at the stables, and we all went up to Doc Halimacek's drugstore for coffee. There was a good-lookin' black-headed girl named Betty working at the fountain. She had been betting some money on Golden Slippers every time the mare ran and was a pretty big winner by now and, needless to say, was overly fond of the little mare.

She heard us talkin' about Golden Slippers dying as we sat around the table. As she was serving us, I rubbed my tired eyes and said, "I don't know why I made a horse doctor."

Betty's eyes flashed and her voice carried a great deal of expression when she looked straight at me and said, "Did ya?"

It was mid-July and there had been some early rain, but the country in general had turned off to be extremely dry by midsummer. Dr. Hoffman, who lived at Marfa, was a very fine old veterinarian who had more or less retired from general practice, had taken on the wholesale distribution of veterinary drugs as his principal business. He was no longer interested in trying to solve the grazing problems of the country and had on several occasions called me to work on cases. This time he was calling about some sheep that were dying about twenty miles south of Marfa. According to his information, there were quite a number of sheep dying or at least sick that were apparently affected the same way in other parts of the Big Bend country south of the Southern Pacific Railroad.

I left Fort Stockton early and was in Marfa by midmorning. We went down to the ranch south of there where the sick sheep were. The rancher had the sheep in a water lot that was probably about five acres in size. I could walk among the sheep and they wouldn't try to run or get away from me, and it would take one of them a long time to cross the lot. They were extremely stiff and were walking in what was generally termed a stilted position, being up on the points of their toes both in front and behind. This flock of sheep were still willing to drink water, but in spite of that fact, they were extremely drawn, though apparently not fevered.

We drove and walked over the pastures where these sheep had been grazing. For the most part the vegetation appeared to be of fair quality, not too dry and still palatable to a sheep. Knowing that a sheep is a green-feeder by choice, and from my experience in poisonous plants, I reasoned that whatever was poisoning the sheep would probably be the vegetation that was greenest and the most protected from the summer sun.

I began to look around the rock ledges and bluffs where there would be a little more shade and perhaps a little more moisture that formed on the rock and ran into the crevices and shallow soil around the rock where something could grow. I found a plant resembling a pea vine that was rather plentiful and was forming some small seed pods— when broken open, I found three or four green peas in them that were in the dough, so to speak. The term "in the dough" means any grain or seed that is in a stage of development and is full of a doughy-like substance that will finally harden when the seed is matured. Such vegetable substances ofttimes contain an unbelievable quantity of acid that in the desert region will more than likely be digestible without any serious upset; the ill effects occur when these substances are carried into the blood stream.

All the time I was pulling these pods and the whole vine too, Dr. Hoffman and I were visitin' and I was explaining to him my theory that this would be the vegetation that was causing the trouble. I put about twenty pounds of vine and seed in a refrigerated box that I had in the back of my car and we drove back to Marfa. I told Dr. Hoffman that I would take the vine to my laboratory and report back to him as soon as possible.

That night I isolated preacyntic acid from the seed, especially from the premature seed. However, it took me another several days before I arrived at the proper prescription to counteract the ill effects of the *garvencia* that had already entered the blood streams of the sheep.

It was after dark and I thought I would take a break

from my laboratory so I walked up the alley and went in the back door of Gallemore's Drugstore. It was Saturday night and the usual Saturday-night business was going on, and I saw Roger Gallemore standing between the ends of two counters up at the front of the store.

A middle-aged widow woman had moved into the country and had leased a ten-section ranch about ten miles west of town where she raised some sheep and goats. Ernie Hamilton, field representative for the National Finance Corporation, whose home office was in Fort Worth, had been this woman's forerunner in arranging for the lease and so forth because she was a customer of the loan company and they were trying to get her in better condition so she could pay out.

She was a pretty tough old ranchwoman, wore men's levi britches and boots nearly all the time, lived hard, was hard-spoken, and was always in hard shape financially, but to-night she had on a nice dress and a lot of make-up. She walked into the drugstore and up to Roger and explained to him that she was having some visitors over this weekend and she thought that they might want a drink of spirits, and since she never went into a whisky store and didn't know anything about that kind of place, she wondered if he would go across the street to Tom's Liquor Store and get her some kind of nice whisky. Of course, old Roger was an easy mark for that kind of a story and said, "Oh sure, what kind do you want, Ma'm?"

"Oh, Mr. Gallemore, anything that you would pick out I'm sure would be all right."

In a few minutes he came back with the quart of whisky in one of those little tight sacks and was carrying it in his left hand under his coat. As he walked in the door, she stepped back and opened a great big purse that you could have put a sack of feed in and Roger caught the hint and sidled up to the purse and dropped the bottle of whisky in it.

The old woman snapped the big purse to and smiled and said, "Just put that on my bill, Mr. Gallemore," as she hurriedly stepped out of the door.

I was in earshot of all this and had seen the little episode, which was very amusing to me. In a few minutes Roger eased up to me and in an unconcerning tone of voice said, "Doc, who was that lady that I was just talking to?"

I said, "Roger, any bootlegger ought to be better acquainted with his customers than that. Who you gonna charge it to?"

Dr. Hoffman was a sincerely religious man and I knew that he had rather not be bothered on Sunday unless it was an emergency, so I waited until Monday morning to go back to Marfa. By this time I had compounded a sufficient quantity of drugs to treat a small flock of sheep. The doctor was busy and didn't go back to the ranch and more or less turned the case and client over to me.

This was the beginning of the successful treatment of sheep poisoned by *garvencia*. As a professional courtesy, I gave Dr. Hoffman the prescription for his future use. However, he said it would be a breach of professional ethics for him to compound it, and thereafter he purchased the prescription from me that he used in his practice.

About an hour before daylight, I pulled away from my office to answer a call about some sick sheep I got during the night from Old Mexico. The first twenty-five or thirty miles west of Fort Stockton is rolling country covered with greasewood, black brush, mesquite, and now and then some flats full of burro grass and other grasses and weeds that make up the forage of that particular strip of country.

I had been getting calls into Old Mexico, and as I started

into the Davis Mountain region still on a good graded road, I couldn't help but dread this call. Between the Davis Mountain Range and the Glass Mountains is high, open rolling prairie country. As I went through this high country and drove into Alpine and on to Marfa, I passed through the south edge of the Davis Mountains. When I turned south at Marfa to go to Presidio, I began to drop from the high country into the rimrock and canyons. The closer to the Rio Grande River I came, the less good forage and the more waste country there was, and from Shafter, an old mining town on Cibolo Creek, to Presidio would not be looked on by most livestock as a lush place to graze.

It was a hundred-and-sixty-five-mile trip to the Rio Grande River; I crossed over the American side at Presidio into Ojinaga on the Mexican side, where I was supposed to meet a Mexican rancher who would show me the way—which turned out to be another ninety miles.

I dreaded this trip for several reasons. The first, I suppose, was because I never got a call to Old Mexico where the time element wasn't involved because of the long wait they made after they needed me and before they called me; then the long distance that I had to drive to get there that always put me in the state of driving under whip hoping that I would not be too late. Another reason was that Old Mexico was far out of my everyday territory and some of the diseases and poisonous-plant troubles were not known to me. Last but not least, when I made such a long call I dreaded the trip back and the calls that would have stacked up while I was gone.

Anyhow, I crossed the river about nine o'clock, not having too much difficulty with the customs officers on either side of the river since they were used to me comin' and goin'. The Mexican ranchero met me at the Bocca Bar. He was a man in his early sixties, very small and slight of build, wearing boots with three-inch heels and a high crown sombrero with an eight-inch brim that made him look nearly as tall as me. A quick glance at his tailored jacket and saddle-cut britches and store-bought shirt told me that he was a stockman and landholder.

As we were about to leave the bar, one of the officers from the Mexican Border Patrol met us at the door with a round-faced, bright-eyed, barefooted Mexican boy about seven or eight years old following him. After a few phrases in Spanish with the old ranchero, he turned to me and in very eloquent English asked if his cousin could ride with us to his casa, which was on our way, about twenty-five miles from the border.

This was fine and the little boy got in the back seat and we heard nothing from him until we came near a little road that turned down the canyon; then he punched the old ranchero and told him in Spanish that this was the place where he wanted off. As he got out of the car, a very ancient truck with solid rubber tires and Presto lights came struggling up the road. He smiled and said that was his papa and ran towards the truck.

On the way to the sheep ranch, the old ranchero described the *malo* (sickness) condition of the *borregas* (sheep). It was late summer and this part of Mexico was having a severe drouth. Even though these bands of sheep were being herded on open range, good vegetation was sparse, and I had a pretty good idea that the sheep had been grazing on a combination of poisonous weeds and vines.

The road got progressively worse for the full ninety miles. We turned several times off of well-traveled roads onto lesser-traveled ones, but none of this was any shock to me since I was used to the road conditions of the country. I was driving a high-wheeled car and had two extra spare tires and an extra tank of gas under the back seat.

We pulled around a high bluff and down in the valley below I saw a typical Mexican sheep camp. There were about twenty acres, I guess, under the south foot of the bluff that had been fenced by hand by laying native stone without any form of cement. This rock fence was tall enough for sheep but would not have held cattle or horses. There was a camp at the foot of the bluff from under which a fair-size spring ran out. A stone wall had been laid around it to protect the spring from the sheep, and the water that ran away from the spring and under the wall down into the draw was left unfenced for the sheep to water. This little camp around the spring was almost a luxury spot to a sheepherder. It had shade from the summer heat, protection from the winter winds, a fair supply of snarly oak trees along the ridge for wood, and an abundance of good cold water.

There were five bands of sheep with fifteen to seventeen hundred in each band. They were taken into the mountains to graze and were not always brought back at night, depending on the distance and the availability of natural water over the rest of the range, which I gathered from conversation was about three hundred thousand acres in American figures.

Since there were so many *malos* (sick sheep), they were all being herded in the nearby hills so that they could be brought to this headquarters corral. Each herder had two dogs, a pack burro, and a riding burro; however, most of their herding was done afoot and the burros were used mostly when they moved camp around over the range. There were about eight thousand sheep in all; more than one third of them showed varying degrees of sickness, and some symptoms were visible on the rest of the sheep.

This was typical of a call to a sheep ranch in Mexico. It had to be of a serious nature and border on what was generally termed a die-out before the Mexican ranchers felt they could stand the expense of a veterinary doctor, since there were very few in that region. I was well acquainted with what to expect and always carried a large supply of any drugs and vaccines that might be needed since it would be such a great distance back to where drugs would be available.

These sheep had a combination of *garvencia* poisoning generally called rattle weed, and a large percentage of those sick showed some signs of having been on lechuguilla.

We ate a noon meal of mutton, frijoles, and tortillas, and the herders washed it down with coffee strong enough to kill while I went to the spring for water two or three times to put out the pepper fire in my belly that helped burn up the grease and frijoles. One reason a white man ought to learn to eat hot pepper is that's what makes those Mexicans able to digest a batch of that stuff that give Gringos indigestion.

There were several hundred sick sheep and a good many dead ones that they were pulling the wool off of near the spring, and to satisfy myself as to my diagnosis, I cut open a few of the sheep that had just died. While we were doing this, the bands of sheep were being brought in from the hills by the herders and their dogs into the rock trap or corral. All the herders were anxious to help doctor the sheep, and they brought them in in small bands into a corner of the fence with the help of the dogs. The dogs would hold the sheep in the corner while the herders would pull the sick ones out by the hind leg. Then they would hold them by the hind leg for me to give hypodermic injections, and I would drench them by the mouth at the same time. Most of these sheep would be saved and this day's work wasn't unusual.

I was hoping I could treat them all at one time and leave

enough medicine so that the herders could continue to treat them after I was gone. It took a great deal of time and patience to show the herders how to drench these sheep and where in the hindquarter to "shoot" them that would get the best results with the least effort, and I was hoping that I might get away from there by late afternoon, in time to cross the river early in the night, which meant that I might get back to my office around midnight.

We had treated all but two hundred head when seven horsemen appeared on the high bluff to the south and west of us about a mile away. The herders noticed them before I did and began to carry on a rather strained conversation in low tones among themselves and they couldn't help but show that there was some anxiety among them.

I didn't speak much Mexican, but I savvied a lot more than I could speak and picked the word *banditos* out of their conversation. The old ranchero who had brought me out and who owned the sheep had paid very little attention to the conversation or to the riders. When we were finished, I said to him, "What do those damn bandits want? Mutton to eat?"

"Doc-tor, they plan, I think, to rob you if you leave here tonight."

"What if I don't leave? You and your herders don't have any guns."

"That is sad, but true, but they would be afraid to enter my camp because General Grearea is my kinsman, and this is known to the Capitán Bandito, but after you leave here, it will be hard for me to guarantee you any protection. For this I am sorry."

I asked in a suspicious tone of voice, "How did they know I was here?"

The old ranchero studied a few minutes and then said, "The officer at the border is a cousin to the Capitán Bandito, and the little boy that rode with us is a cousin to both of them. I am afraid there may be some connection."

I told him I believed I would spend the night and that I knew how we could protect my car and its contents. He didn't know it, but I intended to be some of the contents.

He asked, "How is this, Doc-tor?"

I explained to him that these sick sheep were listless and tired, and it would not be possible to excite them into running by gunfire or riding into them horseback and that we would drive my car out from the spring a piece, and for the herders to bring the sickest of the sheep and bed them down around the car. Then bring the rest of the sheep and bed them down beyond the sick ones. He knew as well as I that neither a horse nor a bandito afoot could wade through that mass of woolly creatures with enough speed to slip up on any of us. The old ranchero seemed to think that this would be all right, and gave instructions in Mexican, and the herders and dogs began to bring the sheep up after I had moved my car.

We ate supper about sundown and were sittin' around the spring a little while before we went to bed. One of the old herders had a very chronic old running sore on his leg just above his knee, and he pulled his britches leg up and showed me the sore by the firelight and wanted some *medicina* to put on it. I told the old ranchero to explain to him that I really needed to scrape out some of those old dead tissues and cause blood to come into the sore in order that the medicino would enter the blood and the tissues to make it get well. Whether the old herder understood this or not, I don't know but he nodded his consent.

I used cocaine to deaden the pain and cleaned out the old wound, which was probably caused by a mesquite thorn or bruise and had been there several years without healing.

I packed it with sulfanilamide powder and put a bandage around his leg and told him to wear it a few days until the sore quit running and scabbed over.

The herders watched very intently and made much comment that I used strong medicine because they could tell from the old herder's expression that there was no pain. One of the young herders spoke up and wanted to show me a tooth, and the old ranchero explained for him that he had been eating on one side of his mouth because this tooth was very sore. When I examined it, I saw the only thing that would help would be to pull it. He asked if he could have some strong medicine before I pulled it. I shot it down with cocaine and got a pair of small horse forceps and the other herders pulled back on his shoulders while I pulled up on the tooth. When it came out, he said in Mexican that it felt much better already. This would be the most medical attention that these Mexican sheepherders ever got and made them to think of me as their friend.

The riders had been gone from sight long enough that we decided we had better make our plans for the night, and I very slowly picked my way through about three hundred yards of sick sheep to my car. Just at dark I heard some commotion back up at the spring among the herders. It developed that one of the banditos had been sent in to tell the ranchero that they wanted my spare tires from the car and all the American dollars I brought with me and that I could go tonight or tomorrow without any fear.

The old ranchero waded through the sheep with this messenger, who was maybe nineteen years old, slick-faced, wearing two big *pistolas,* big spoke rowel spurs, a ragged white cotton shirt and ragged, what were once white, cotton britches. He was not a big Mexican and didn't have a tough face or voice.

The rancher spoke English and told me what the proposition from the banditos amounted to, and I asked, "What makes them think I've got any fear now?"

Since the bandito was only the messenger and neither spoke nor understood English, I was at a great advantage. I told the ranchero, while I searched around for my money and got my keys to unlock the turtle of my car to get the spare tires for him, to call two herders to come help carry the spare tires through the sheep. He hollered at his herders in Mexican and explained why I wanted them, and even in the dark you could see this young bandito was well pleased and had begun to get real brave.

By the time the herders were about fifty feet away, I had filled a 50-cc. syringe with calcium gluconate and had put a two-inch 16-gauge needle on the hub of the syringe during the time I was pretending to get the spare tire out of the back of the car. At the right moment I told the ranchero for him and the herders to surprise the bandito and overpower him, and then I would give him a shot of *real stout* medicine.

Mr. Bandito had become so relaxed and so sure of himself that it was easy for the herders to sneak up behind him, throw him to the ground, and tie his hands behind his back while the ranchero jerked his pistols away from their scabbards. Of course, the calcium gluconate wouldn't hurt a sheep or a Mexican either, but that two-inch 16-gauge needle and the mass of calcium gluconate being forced into the muscle structure was painful when I jabbed him in the thigh with it.

While I was doing this, I told the ranchero to tell him that this would give him the disease of the sheep, and he would give it to the rest of the banditos when we turned him loose, and in a little while we would be rid of them all. When I jabbed him with that big needle, he howled at the top of his voice, and as he got up and stumbled back through the sheep when we turned him loose, he was hollerin' to the other banditos to bring him his horse.

We had a big laugh, sat around awhile in the dark, and all of us pretended to go to bed. It's not often that sick, fevered, vomiting sheep smell good, but that bunch smelled real good around my car till morning.

Most of the sheep were lots better the next morning, and I left plenty of medicine for them to be treated as long as they needed it. The ranchero thought he would help keep the banditos off by going back with me. He got out at the bar, and I drove on down to the port of entry at the bridge.

When one of the Mexican officers at the port of entry looked into the back of my car, he showed considerable shock that I still had both spare tires, had a pocketful of money to pay my fee, and was still wearing my gold watch. This couldn't have bothered him any more than it did me, wondering how the grapevine worked from the Mexican boy to the banditos.

There was a little slack in my practice, which was usual in the late summer, and I was trying to shape up my own horse business. I had a good many mares and colts scattered around, pasturing them with different ranchers, and I had made a deal with Con and Concho Cunningham for some more mares.

These mares, with the exception of one, were all smooth-mouthed and up to eighteen years old. The filly colts were left on the mares in the deal and were great big colts, ready to be cut off. We had these mares in the railroad stockpens in Fort Stockton and were roping the colts and dragging them out of the pen when Gid Reding rode up.

Gid was an old-time cowboy who had gained fame, if not notoriety, for having some sort of a peculiar kinship with animals. He broke the worst of outlaw horses to ride, and

Banditos

they never bucked with him. Nobody's guard dog would bite him; instead they would wag their tail and come up and meet him, and they would carry on some type of conversation. Horses had no fear of Gid, and he could walk into a band of wild mares and rub around over them and pull their tails and get on one if he wanted to. Gid always swore that he never knew what it was about him that caused him to get along with animals, and I guess he was telling the truth because I never knew what it was about me and other people that caused us to put up with him.

He came into the corral and bemeaned and reprimanded us for draggin' his "little friends" around at the end of a nasty rope, and after sufficiently bemeanin' us for our brutality and ignorance in no uncertain terms, he walked in among the mares and colts and what he said to them, I'll never know, but they must have liked it.

They nuzzled around on him and he pulled the mares' tails, played with the colts, and in a few minutes he came walking out of the bunch of horses with his arm over a colt's neck, talking to him. They seemed to be having a very enjoyable visit as they strolled out of the corral into the next pen, where I was holding the gate open. When Gid turned around to walk back into the pen, the colt, believe it or not, turned and tried to follow him, with me standing there tryin' to shut the gate.

In a short time, Gid had all the colts "visited" away from the mares and into the other pen. He remarked that one mare in there particularly appealed to his fancy. She was a seven-year-old outlaw mare that didn't have a colt—a nice, big, black half-thoroughbred-looking mare with white markings.

I told Gid that he was welcome to the mare if he would like to have her, so he walked over into the bunch of horses, scratched around on this particular mare, who was known to be an outlaw and had hurt a few cowboys, and in a few minutes we looked around and saw Gid sitting on top of the mare, no rope, no bridle, no nothin'. He said he didn't believe he would take her, but that he was glad to make her acquaintance.

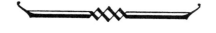

MRS. ROSE,
MR. ROSE-
POISON HAY

Several times during my late summer and fall practice, an occasional cow would be found dead in an alfalfa field. It was the practice of alfalfa farmers after they baled their last cutting of hay to start grazing the alfalfa stubbles until cold weather. Each time I was called for one of these cases, I would find no apparent sickness in the rest of the herd, and the cow that had died would be lying down in a normal resting position with her legs under her and head laid back on her shoulders. There was never any sign of a death struggle on the ground.

When doing post-mortems on this kind of a case I would find an enlargement of the spleen and discoloration of the

liver, and these indications were the usual symptoms found in the contagious disease of anthrax. However, it was common knowledge that you never have just one case of anthrax. It is a spore disease and spreads rapidly through a herd and cattle would die in bunches. This evidence was kept so we wouldn't start a scare. These scattered cases through the years caused me some unrest but there had been so few of them that they had not been a serious part of my practice.

In late September, Alton Simmons, who farmed and ranched north of Fort Stockton on the Pecos River near Imperial, called me late one afternoon. His tone of voice almost reached a stage of excitement when he said that he had two cows dead and two more down. From his description it seemed to me to be a recurrence of that same trouble I had not yet been able to solve.

I got to his place a little before dark, and we cut open one of the dead cows to look at the vital organs and intestinal tract. Here again was the same enlarged spleen and discolored liver. I treated the two cows that were down, and they offered no resistance when we took hold of them. They had no fever and did not appear to be too sick, except that they refused to get up.

I didn't know what I was treating and used a shotgun remedy for general poisoning and told Alton, "I'm only trying and haven't positively diagnosed what's the matter with the cattle."

By daylight the next morning he called to tell me that both cows had died and there was another showing signs of sickness. I hurried out. I tried a different medication on this cow. However, before I gave the cow any medication, I took a sterile syringe and drew a 500-cc. vial full of blood and sealed it for later analysis in my laboratory.

Alton looked at the amount of blood that I pulled out

of the jugular vein and said, "Doc, be careful that you don't drink some of that stuff. You ain't the best vet I ever saw, but you're the only one we got."

I asked Alton what he was feeding these cattle, and he told me that they were grazing in the field and he wasn't feeding them any sack feed.

For want of better information, I told Alton that I thought these cattle were being poisoned by fertilizer and asked him about the possibility of some used fertilizer sacks being scattered around the field. He said that this couldn't be—that the land had not been fertilized for two years.

The cattle were drinking from the irrigation ditch that ran through the field. There couldn't be anything wrong with that water because cattle all over the district were drinking from that same irrigation ditch and these were the only sick ones. This case, like many others in my veterinary practice, caused me to be as much of a detective as a doctor.

Alton had over a hundred cattle in this field and he was losing from one to three cows every twenty-four hours without any apparent sickness in the rest of the herd grazing around where we were treating the sick and the dying. He was a heavy-set, good-natured, middle-aged fellow who had always worked hard and these losses were hurting. He said, "Doc, I sure hope that you find out pretty soon what's killin' these cattle 'cause I've bragged on you so much to the neighbors, I would hate to have to buy some more cattle for you to finally prove to them I'm not lying."

I hadn't been able to isolate any toxic substance in the blood samples I had been collecting. One night I took a 100-cc. vial of blood from a cow that was dying, drove to the airport at Midland, and shipped it packed in ice to my good friend in New York City who was recognized as an outstanding analytical chemist. I knew my limitations in chemical research and had always thought it was smart to know people who knew things I didn't and I developed good contacts in all fields of research.

By noon the next day I had a wire from my friend telling me that there were five hundred times more nitrates in the blood than is normal for any domestic animal.

I drove out to Alton's and showed him the wire. We walked the field out in sections and didn't find anything of a foreign nature that could possibly have any agricultural or industrial nitrogens. As we came to the irrigated ditch on the east side of the field, I noticed Alton had moved his fence before the last cutting of alfalfa. There was a strip across the ditch that had been hard to get to with machinery, and he had neglected cutting it the last time he baled hay.

This alfalfa was tall and ragged because the cattle had tromped through. It was not as tender as the alfalfa that had been cut, and probably only a few head would graze across the ditch. The blooms were completely gone and the seed pods on this alfalfa were almost mature.

I started stripping the seed off the stalk by hand and told Alton that I needed several ounces to use for laboratory testing. We gathered more than enough and put it in our coat pockets. When we got to the car, we emptied it into a paper sack and I went to my laboratory.

By now it was night and I started to work on the samples we had gathered. This almost mature alfalfa seed that was slightly soft was hot with nitric acids that when fully matured would become various forms of nitrate sulfates. I woke Alton up about midnight and showed him what I had found, and we moved the cattle to another pasture in the night until he could cut and destroy that strip of alfalfa that had gone to seed.

When I got back to town I stopped at the Hollywood

Café, the only all-night café. It was a pretty tough place and you were taking chances with your health if you ordered anything that was more open than a bottle drink or a hard-boiled egg. However, since it was the only all-night place, I would go in occasionally.

As I went in, I noticed a rough-looking character asleep with his head on the table. Sometime earlier in the night he had ordered a combination salad, and the waitress had brought it out and put it on the table. By the time he woke up, he was probably a little closer to being sober than when he came in.

During the lapse of time, this combination salad had wilted down to where it had come apart, and the oil had dropped out of the dressing. He called the waitress over and pointed to the salad and in a whisky tone of voice said, "Have I or should I?"

As I left, I realized that the human race might also get poisoned on bad green feed.

On my way back to my laboratory, I wondered why such alfalfa seed had never been suspected of being poisonous before. Later in conversation with people who raised alfalfa seed to be used for planting, I learned that rats would not eat them and would rarely ever cut a seed sack. I couldn't get rabbits or guinea pigs to eat the matured seed in any mixture that I tried. The only creature I ever found that would readily eat alfalfa seed were baby chicks that had not been hatched more than a few days before, and they would fall over dead in the matter of an hour or less if they filled up on them.

There are several medical agents that can counteract the effects of nitrates, and there are medical and chemical properties that can neutralize nitrates when they are present in the digestive tract, so the search for treatment was neither a serious nor a time-consuming matter. Dr. Udall of Cornell University had described nitrate poisoning from other vegetable sources and especially from wilted green-cut oats as early as 1925, but to the best of my knowledge, up until the case of Alton Simmons's cows, alfalfa seed had never been thought of as containing poison substances.

Back in the summer, Hart Johnson, one of the town's native sons and a prominent lawyer, had taken his wife and daughter, Robin, on vacation. Mrs. Rose, their neighbor, whose house faced east on the street opposite them, kept Robin's little female dog while they were gone.

Mrs. Rose had taught school for fifty years or so, ran a village newspaper for another fifty or so, and this last fifty she spent tending to other people's business. She was a little bitty sharp-tongued old woman, and she thought how nice it would be for me to spay Robin's dog while she was gone.

I wasn't particularly interested in performing any small-animal surgery, but being the village horse doctor and the only one for a hundred miles or more, I inherited this kind of practice. There was no talking Mrs. Rose out of doing the little dog's operation, so I performed it in the back of my office and delivered the little dog to Mrs. Rose wrapped in a blanket before she came out from under the influence of anesthesia.

I explained to Mrs. Rose in detail that I had made a lateral incision in the skin only and had parted the muscles of the abdominal cavity with my fingers and there had been no muscles severed. The purpose of this explanation was to show the old woman that there was no real strain on the four stitches I had taken to close the incision in the skin of the little dog's belly, and if the dog tore the stitches out or when they rotted and came loose, there was no serious damage and she should not worry about the incision opening up.

About four or five days after that, I stopped by the drug-store and I was told that Mrs. Rose had called for me. I went on up to the café to eat dinner, and they told me Mrs. Rose had called. Call her. At Dee Walker's filling station, they said Mrs. Rose had been by and said for me to call her!

When I got to my office, I thought it best to get Mrs. Rose out of the way so I called her and after fifteen minutes of constant flow of the English language from her, I gathered that one stitch had broken and she was seriously request-ing that I come by and look, so I said I would. There was no damage done and the little dog was healing nicely. I again explained to her the unimportance of these stitches and told her if the rest broke to think nothing about it.

The next day from nine to five wherever I stopped in town, somebody would say, "Oh, yes, Mrs. Rose wants you to come by." This procedure went on for four stitches and two weeks until I gave the old woman a gentlemanly sort of cussin'. The dog, other than the anxiety of Mrs. Rose, had an uneventful recovery and Robin came home and went to playing with her little dog without knowin' that she had ever been operated on.

Mr. Rose was a fine old gentleman, very obedient, cowed, subdued, and sometimes, I imagine, fearful of existence, who was always well dressed and well spoken. He was the haybarn manager for the Alfalfa Growers' Association. On the first cold morning that fall, Mr. Rose stopped me on the street. He was tall and dignified and wore a long overcoat which made him look even taller. After he had spoken very gentlemanly, he said, "Doctor, there is a very serious matter that I must confront you with."

I said in an unconcerned tone of voice, "Mr. Rose, life can't always be pleasant. What's the trouble?"

He was trying to fill his pipe with one finger and was

nervously stuffing the tobacco in the bowl. He gazed across the street and said in a broken voice, "I regret to have to take this matter up with you."

I insisted that he get it off his chest and tell me what his trouble was, so maybe I could help. He momentarily stopped packing his pipe and glanced at me and said in a very shaky voice, "I am told that you have made disparaging remarks about Mrs. Rose."

"Well, Mr. Rose, I'll tell you verbatim what I said, if that would help."

After a moment of silence, he said, "Doctor, that might be the proper beginning."

"Mr. Rose, I don't know that you would call it disparaging but the statement I made back in the summer was, 'Mrs. Rose would provoke Jesus Christ to use profanity.' "

He turned his pipe over and started tryin' to beat some of the tobacco out where it would light, and after a long silence he said, in a very relaxed tone, "I hardly feel that I can take exception to that statement. Good day, Doctor."

The acreage in the valleys around Fort Stockton that was irrigated from natural springs was planted mostly with alfalfa. This year had been a good hay year and most of the farmers had gotten five cuttings of good leafy alfalfa and the farmers' co-op haybarns in Fort Stockton were full. Since it was early winter, hay had begun to move, and the manager, Mr. Rose, was doing a good job of moving the year's production.

I was called to the Iron Mountain Ranch that was operated by Buck Pyle as a part of the West-Pyle Livestock Company. The foreman there was a fellow by the name of Carter, a good rancher who took an interest in taking the best care of his horses. When I got there, I was confronted with a horse that had just died and there were several sick in the corral.

I did a post-mortem on the horse and examined the rest of the horses that were affected. It was a very simple case of arsenic poisoning. Since these horses were only being fed alfalfa hay, it would be readily suspected of carrying some arsenic poisoning. The most common form of this sort of agricultural poisoning would be the presence of Paris green, which was used in dusting and spraying cotton and other crops to protect them against insects.

Carter took the horses off this hay and put them on other feed, and no more of them died or got sick. I carried a bale of the hay back with me to my laboratory and washed out and identified by laboratory processes the presence of arsenic. I called Carter and told him what I had found, and the news spread fast that there was some poison in some of the Fort Stockton hay.

Within a matter of a day, Mr. Rose had had several people refuse to take delivery on hay, and Mr. Rhodes, the banker, and I were discussing the damage that my diagnosis had done to the Fort Stockton hay market. They called the county agent in for a consultation. He in turn came and questioned me about the accuracy of my laboratory techniques in finding the arsenic. He wasn't a bad fellow and had the banker and the farmers on him, and, of course, he was definitely on their side—if there were to be sides.

The next day Mr. Rhodes and Mr. Rose called me into the bank to explain to me what the hay crop meant to the economy of Pecos County and to the bank deposits of Fort Stockton.

By now I had been there several years and had lots of practice and at this particular season I was overworked, short of rest, and short of patience, so without sittin' down in that mahogany chair, I proceeded to give them all a pretty quick, fair cussin' by telling them that I wasn't runnin' the bank, I didn't have a hay crop, I wasn't runnin' the co-op haybarn, and I damn sure didn't aspire to be the county agent, and there would be no retraction from me as to the content of the poison in the hay that I analyzed, which was the cause of the death of the horse that I did the post-mortem on. I told them if they were particularly interested in clearin' the matter up in order to best represent the interest of the hay growers, it would be well to determine which farmer's hay had been delivered to the Iron Mountain Ranch and his lot of hay should be examined and if necessary destroyed, and I respectfully reminded them that I did not say all the hay in the haybarn was poisoned, but that the hay fed the horses of the West-Pyle Livestock Company was damn sure poisoned. I told them in clear, clean language that before I changed my diagnosis, the flames of hell would be as cold as a strawberry popsicle. With that closing remark, I stormed out of the bank.

After this session was over, they determined that the hay belonged to the Hayes Brothers. The county agent and Mr. Rose from the haybarn asked them whether or not they had used any poison on their farm that could have gotten into the hay. They strongly denied having had any crops poisoned or dusted and decided that they ought to sue me. Well, this brought up the possibility that whoever had gotten poisoned hay might be ready to sue them and make the hay company a part to the suit. So in a few days Mr. Rhodes, the banker, asked me what my testimony would be in the case of a law suit. He was being very smooth about it and tried hard not to upset my disposition. Well, my disposition was already upset, and I told him to file suit and find out.

I thought at the time that if there were any more poisoned horses on some other ranch that a suit might develop, but Buck Pyle was prominent in political affairs and

fair in 'most all matters and I'm sure didn't want the publicity nor the unpleasantness of a law suit. This kind of
stuff was talked around up and down the street and some
of the hay farmers threatened to do without my services,
which didn't bother me a damn bit, and these rumors and
unpleasant conversation went on most of the winter.

It is characteristic of the Trans-Pecos Region of Texas to
have high, hard winds especially in February and March.
At this time there was an airfield for flight training at Fort
Stockton and there was a gathering of flight instructors
from several other points. Among the social events that
were staged to entertain the visiting instructors, some of
the townspeople had a big barbecue in Rooney Park.

All the single gals in town had a date with a visiting
flight instructor, and me and my gal friend were invited
to the affair. She was a secretary for an oil company in Fort
Stockton, and it happened in conversation over the barbecue that night that there was a fellow in the group that she
had known in high school. We were at the same table
visitin' and eatin' and they were reminiscing about their
school days. It was a very relaxed atmosphere and I supposed that caused him to make the comment, "I won't forget the last time I was in Fort Stockton."

Of course she asked him, "Why?" and he went into detail and in the presence of a female audience I'm sure
dressed up the story some and began to tell us about his
experience as a crop duster the year before. He said the
Hayes Brothers had hired him to come in to dust their cotton crop with arsenic dust.

We were eating outside on benches in the park and the
wind was high and he said that was what reminded him
of the story. When he got up in the air that day, as he

tripped his equipment to release the dust on the cotton crop, there had been a big downwind and blew the poison way off course from where he had intended to put it.

Up to now I had done nothing but listen and eat barbecue, but when this flyer mentioned turning that arsenic dust loose, I throwed my head up and turned an ear. I whispered to my gal friend to question him a little further, and he very readily gave out with all the information. We invited him and his date to come to my office with us and finish out the festivities.

I had some good Scotch whisky, which was rare during the war years and which I never drank, and I felt that this might be the right place to pour it out. I poured the Scotch into 500-cc. glass beakers and they didn't water it down too much while I watched them and asked him more questions. Nobody got drunk, but Mr. Flyer got willin' after I told my story and asked him to stay over next morning and meet with me, the banker, and Mr. Rose.

He evidently didn't have any ill effects from the evening before and true to his word showed up at my office at nine o'clock. We went to the bank, and I introduced him to Mr. Rhodes and asked him if he would call Mr. Rose to come down. In a few minutes I presented my evidence to them as to where the Paris green arsenic came from and who employed this cropduster, which put Mr. Rhodes and Mr. Rose into quite a state of shock as to the honor and integrity of the Hayes Brothers.

The possibility of law suits and the question of my diagnosis suddenly died. The Hayes Brothers and others began to be awful nice to me in hopes I might forget about the whole incident, and there was a greater respect for my professional opinion that suddenly prevailed around the damn bank.

STRONG MEDICINE

Early in April I was in Pecos, Texas, tending to some land business and I dropped by the lobby of the Brandon Hotel to visit with Buck Jackson in his office, which was the gathering ground for loafin' stockmen. After a few "Hidy's" and light conversation, I told Buck that I needed to get back to Fort Stockton. Maybe somebody had some trouble with their livestock while I was gone and I could take up the slack in the money I'd been spending during the day.

As I was about to leave, Old Man Sanhill, who stuttered pretty bad, came up and we shook hands. After a polite remark or two, he started changin' feet and stompin' the tile lobby floor tryin' to get around to quizzin' me about a

horse he had. When he finally came to the question he said, "I-I got a c-c-olt that's s-s-she-ddin' his two-year-old t-t-t-eeth t-too early, and I-I'm a-a-fra-id it might s-s-s-tunt his growth. I wonder i-i-if there is s-s-s-ome-t-thin' you could give him that would k-k-k-eep them front baby t-t-t-eeth from comin' out s-so s-s-s-oon."

"Mr. Sanhill, I never heard of any colt shedding his first teeth before he was two years and six months old. This means that those two front permanent teeth will be grown at three years old."

This made him nervous and as he stomped and stuttered, he explained to me that he knowed when the colt was born that the old mare had had a colt once before that shed its teeth too soon, and he was afraid that this would stunt this colt's growth.

I said, "No, when any horse gets part of his permanent teeth, he can bite off grass and chew feed better and he'll grow faster, and if that old mare always has a colt that sheds its teeth too early, you better keep her. However, in my years in the horse business and in general practice, I've never seen a case like this."

He insisted that what he was telling me was the facts and since he lived on the road between there and Fort Stockton, he wished I'd stop on the way back and look at the colt's mouth. He was figurin' that this wouldn't be a call, and I would give him some information free. I don't know what his real plans were for the day, but he said, "I-I'm goin' home right now, and I-I-'ll be t-t-here when you s-s-s-top."

I drove up in front of Old Stutter's shack and it was a typical camp for an oldtime race-horseman who raced on the brush tracks. There were half a dozen single stalls built wide apart from each other with separate corrals around each one and a little half-mile training track scraped off in the pasture behind the two-room shack and the stalls.

He had this young horse haltered and led out into the yard. I got out of the car and Old Stutter began intendin' to make me know that this was just a comin' two-year-old and not a comin' three-year-old that would be shedding his teeth. I noticed at a glance that there was no colt curl left in the hair of the tail and he had roached his mane. The forearms and stifles were showing more muscular develop-ment than would be found on a two-year-old.

While I was takin' all this in, I opened the colt's mouth and the two baby teeth in front in the lower jaw had already shed out and the permanent teeth were barely breaking the gums. This was not a colt and was going to have a firm three-year-old mouth by midsummer. I told Old Stutter that from what he said, it was a freak, but it looked normal to me and the only knowledge I had of a horse's mouth was how to develop teeth, not how to keep them from growin'.

He followed me to the car stutterin' and slobberin' and tellin' me that until he found a horse doctor that knew something, he was going to put this here colt on "soft" feed. As I drove the rest of the way home, I tried to figure out why Old Stutter would want that young horse to be a two-year-old, but the only answer that crossed my mind was maybe he was trying to switch registration papers that he had that would fit a two-year-old that he had sold or has possibly died.

A few days later an oil-field worker from over close to Crane called and asked me if I could do anything to help straighten a young horse's feet. After some conversation, I told him if it wasn't an urgent call, I would come by his barn in the next few days and look at the horse. This was all right with him.

I made it by there before the week was over. He had a nice, well-built two-year-old filly that had good body conformation except for her left foreleg from the knee to the ground, and she was a little low at the withers. The leg was turned at the knee joint outward and when she moved, the foot was way out of line with the back foot on the same side.

I explained to him that this was what was termed as a splay foot and was caused by the twist in the knee that he hadn't noticed. I told him that it would need to be trimmed to cause the foot to come to the ground level, but that it could never be turned by any means to where she would travel straight on it.

He said, "Doc, this filly is bred to knock a hole in the wind, and I sure did want to run her in that Fourth of July two-year-old race over on the edge of New Mexico. The entrance fee is $100 and the tracks are adding $1,000 to the purse."

"That leg will never stand the strain of racin', and I wouldn't spend the money that it would take to get her ready knowin' that she might break that leg."

As I left his barn, it dawned on me why Old Stutter was trying to keep the baby teeth in that three-year-old horse's mouth: a three-year-old would be so much better developed for a race when the rest of the horses would only be two years old.

When I left Crane, I drove on to Midland, where I was to do work on some horses' teeth and do a little surgery on some horses' backs. While I was in this man's stable, he brought a fat, overkept two-year-old filly out of the stall and said, "Doc, I've paid the entrance fee on this filly for that New Mexico two-year-old race, and we're goin' to start training her right away. But, she's pigeon-toed in front, and I was wondering how to shoe her to help her front feet."

"That won't be too big a chore. You cut the wall of the inside of the foot down and round out the toe and leave as much of the outside wall as possible. You see, it's not the feet that are actually crooked in the filly's make-up. She has a swinging pastern from her ankle to her foot that is crooked, and that causes the foot to hit the ground with more pressure on the outside and wear down, and with less pressure on the inside, the length of the walls of the foot don't stay even with the outside that's catchin' the weight."

"That sure makes sense, and I never knew before that the trouble was in the pastern and not in the foot."

As I looked at the filly, I realized that she had beautiful slopin' shoulders, a short back, and powerful hindquarters and was not low in front. I said, "She sure looks like a fireball."

He told me about the winners in her bloodline and said he had high hopes for this filly if he could keep her sound, and that they would follow my instructions on the front feet.

The next day a fellow hauled a two-year-old colt to my office from Orla, which was right up on the line of New Mexico. He unloaded a good-lookin' chestnut colt with a lot of body, an honest two-year-old mouth, and a badly sickled pair of hocks. He said he was training the colt for the race over in the edge of New Mexico on the Fourth of July and that the colt had "sored up" in his hind legs.

This old boy wasn't dumb and he said, "Doc, I know his hocks ain't good, but I wondered if there was some kind of a rub or maybe even a blister that would tighten his hocks up to where he could run a few races."

"Yeah, I can furnish you a good liquid liniment and if you use it lightly every day, it's a tightener. If you rub it too much or put it under bandage, it's a blister. Since you're a horseman, I'll furnish you with the liniment and you use it the way you see fit."

A few days before the last of April, Juan came in my

office. He had been raised and worked on ranches around Fort Stockton and had a new job as foreman on a ranch just over the line in New Mexico. After a short visit he said, "Doc, you know de colt I raise from my Monte Cordor mare and your stud you got, heem is just a leetle bit too young to run theese other two year old what will be in theese race July 4. I sure theenk he might outrun the other colts preety bad, but he needs to get some more big on heem before theen."

"Juan, I remember when you brought the mare to the stud in November and that colt should have been born in late October, but I've never seen him."

"I weesh you would come to see heem. Maybe so you tell if he ween that $1,000 what I need so bad."

The deadline to enter a two-year-old in the race was May 1 and time was running short, so I told Juan I would be by his place late the next day.

Horses all have their birthdays on the first day of January, so far as racing purposes are concerned. If a foal is born as late as December 31, for racing-record purposes, it will be a year old the next morning, January 1. This is the reason that all breeders raising racing horses try to breed their mares to foal as soon after the first day of January as possible so that the next January when the colt is considered a year old, he will almost be a year old. Then when the second January passes, this same colt races as a two-year-old until the third January.

This explains why many horses in a two-year-old race can be closer to three years old, and it's easy to see the handicap that a late colt would be racing under. Several months in the second year of a colt's life can make a great deal of difference in his size and development. This is the reason that Juan was worried about getting some more "big" on his colt.

When I drove up, the mare that was the mother of this colt was in the front yard. She was an outstanding mare and a family pet and was nursing a new baby colt. Juan's flock of small children were playing with the colt and crawlin' around on the old mare, and the baby that was just old enough to walk was holdin' on to her tail to stand up. This is the kind of a mare that money can't buy and will live in the memory of those children.

The colt that Juan had talked to me about was in the back yard behind the house and every time he nickered, the old mare would still answer him even though she had a new baby colt. Juan said she was so gentle that she had never weaned him and would still let him suck on one side while the baby colt sucked on the other and so he had to keep him in the back yard.

We sat on the back porch and looked at the colt. He was a glossy seal-brown color with no white markings on his feet and legs and just a few white hairs in his forehead. He was small because of his age; however, he was perfectly sound in his legs and his body was ideally proportioned for balance and speed, and for his size he had an unbelievably deep girth that housed big lungs and a strong heart.

Juan talked about the $100 entrance fee and said that he had it saved up and he would sure like to win that $1,000 purse. I told Juan to put his money down and enter the colt and I would prescribe some strong medicine, and if he would train and feed and take care of the colt, he would have a good chance of winnin'.

Juan was a hard-workin' young man with a large family of small children. He was a good citizen and fair in his thinking and didn't intend to do anything to win the race except to do the best job of training and caring for his colt that he could. According to my acquaintance with brush-track racemen, his intentions were far more honorable than most, and I was glad to be helping him develop a race horse that was sired by my stallion.

In the next few weeks, I saw Old Stutter several times and he would barely grunt as he passed me. I would've asked him if he was training his two-year-old, but if I had he would have lied, so I didn't mention it.

I was in Crane several times and they were training the splay-footed filly. When I saw her in late June, it looked like they were about to make a dummy out of me because she was training good and musclin' up as much as a two-year-old can, and that crooked leg hadn't given her any trouble.

Then I saw the bad-hocked horse up at Orla one time, and the man told me that the liniment as a rub had quit doing enough good and he had finally put a blister on the horse's hocks and wrapped them under bandages. When I watched the colt move, it seemed there was no pain in his hind legs.

I hadn't had an occasion to see the pigeon-toed horse that I told the owner corrective shoeing would probably help. Anywhere that race-horse men gathered, the conversation would soon turn to the race for two-year-olds the Fourth of July.

I went by Juan's on an average of once a week to see how he was comin' along with his colt, which he had named Pronto. One time when I was there he was feeding Pronto a little corn in his feed, and I told him to take the corn out and to feed him clean dried oats and be sure that he got his strong medicine. As he trained the colt and gave him the best of care, I continued to emphasize that Pronto shouldn't get his medicine until he finished the day's training.

On another visit Juan was so anxious to get some more

"big" on Pronto that he had bought some horse sweet feeds, and I had to explain to him that this might cause Pronto to not want to take his medicine and to put him back on dry clean oats and good hay. Juan was always grateful and very obedient in carryin' out my instructions. He trained Pronto late every afternoon when he had finished his ranch work, and his whole family was counting the days until the big race.

The Fourth of July is celebrated by various patriotic festivities and ceremonies across the United States, but in the West there are two great patriotic forms of entertainment—rodeos and horse races—and the flag-waving is done by the winners.

There is just one kind of weather on the Fourth of July in the West—hot, dry, and windy. The natives and the horses thrive on it. Being wet with sweat and covered with dust is not out of style at a rodeo or horse race and anyone that complains is a tourist, a newcomer, or a weakling. High-heeled boots, tight-legged duckin' britches, loud shirts, and big hats were the most stylish attire for kids just older than cradle size all the way to the grandpas and grandmas. Anybody wearin' low quarters or a white shirt and was bareheaded was bound to be a stranger.

There were to be other races during the day for horses of various ages, colors, and sizes, but the race for two-year-olds caused more conversation than all the rest. The crowd gathered at the track early in the morning and there was a fair amount of racin', bettin', winnin', and losin' by noon.

A brush racetrack is usually the product of local racehorse owners and some small-town Chamber of Commerce or other civic organization. The track will be graded out of an open spot in somebody's pasture and usually not over three fourths of a mile long. A committee of local citizens sets up rules that are supposed to be abided by, but there is actually no legal supervision of the conduct of racing conditions that are enforceable at a brush racetrack. There may be a few stalls and other buildings and in some cases a small grandstand, but, for the most part, the race-horse fans line the fence of the track and most onlookers would like to be as close to the finish line as possible.

There's just one kind of grub at a Western outdoor festivity: namely, barbecued beef, beans, 'taters, and bread with black coffee and other strong drink. It usually takes about two hours of this part of the day for the kids to get their clothes nasty and the grown folks to stretch out in the shade and try to get over the mornin's doin's.

Juan brought his whole family and all of his horses in his pickup truck and stopped just beyond the finish line. Close to two thirty the first race of the afternoon called was for the two-year-olds. As Juan led Pronto away from the pickup, the smaller children were rubbin' and talkin' to him and the old mare was standing tied to the pickup and the little colt was wanderin' around with the kids. As Juan's son, Pedro, rode Pronto and Juan led him away from the pickup, the old mare and Pronto carried on a lot of conversation in high nickerin' horse tones.

The two-year-olds were brought out into a fenced-off spot and the race committee went over them to see if they were all eligible to run. There were eight entered in the race and as the committee went through and inspected them, they found Old Stutter's two-year-old colt to be a three-year-old horse and began to explain and later try to convince him that his three-year-old horse could not be entered in a two-year-old race. There was a hell of an argument and a fair cuss fight but no blood was shed, and I doubt seriously from the toughness of the characters that anybody's feelings were hurt. The rest of the two-year-olds were declared

eligible and were being saddled and gettin' ready for the
start of the race.

This was a race of five hundred yards, which is just a
little over a quarter of a mile. The pigeon-toed two-year-old
from Midland had been drawn down into good racing flesh
and condition and her feet had been improved a whole lot
by shoein'. The splay-footed two-year-old was still splay-
footed, and the bad-hocked chestnut had been blistered
until the hair was all off of his hocks, but he traveled and
showed no pain. There were three others I had never seen
before that all appeared to be in racing condition, and
Pronto was as ready for a race as any little horse could
ever be.

The jockeys were quite an assortment of ages and sizes.
Juan's thirteen-year-old son, Pedro, was a small boy and
an ideal jockey for Pronto. There was a little bitty dried-up
old Indian who would have had to have been over seventy
jockeying the pigeon-toed horse. The rest were in-between
ages and sizes. One boy, who was ridin' the splay-footed
filly, looked like he would weigh one hundred and fifty
pounds, which was awful heavy for a jockey and especially
for a two-year-old.

The seven head were standing on a line drawn across
the track and were to run to the finish line, where the
crowd gathered. When Pronto was lined up with the rest
of the starting line, he nickered plaintively and the old
mare answered him in very strong motherly tones. It was
easy to see that he was younger and much smaller than
the other horses. However, he was to a horseman the best
made, the soundest, and in the most perfect racing condition with good manners and proud of his little jockey.

When the starting judge fired the pistol and the race was
on, Pronto broke out of the pack neck in neck with the

pigeon-toed horse from Midland. Since nobody had thought the little horse had a chance to win, the crowd went wild. When Pronto remembered the strong medicine that he got at the end of every race, the closer he got, the faster he went, and he left the Midland horse behind. At the finish line, he was four lengths ahead.

About the time he stuck his nose over the finish line, a loud noise was heard down the track that sounded like a shot; the splay-footed filly had broke a leg. The other horses were scattered out between the Midland horse and the crippled filly. Pronto nickered real loud and Pedro didn't try to hold him back as he rushed up to the old mare and went to nursin' that STRONG MEDICINE that I had been prescribing all during trainin'.

All my life my first interest has been and still is horses. For a number of years I had been interested in the color of horses. Horses do not breed true to color—a mare and a stallion may produce a foal much lighter or much darker than themselves. During mankind's efforts to improve horses by selection, there have been very few cases where any stability of color has been possible in a breed, and there has never been a breed of horses that run true to a definite color without exception. This fact and other oddities about horse color caused me to develop an interest in the research on the color of horses.

The West had thousands of brood mares and other range horses in herds owned by individuals with as few as forty or fifty head and one of the largest horse ranches in the Trans-Pecos Region had four thousand head as late as the early fifties. Many of the horses in the Far Southwest had good blood infused in them, and there was quite an array of colors and shades available, which made the research of color interesting to "play" with when I had the time to spare away from my general practice.

Sometimes I would find a horse of a good solid color and clip hair from different parts of his body and take a sample from his mane and tail. I would run these various specimens through my laboratory tests and by various chemical methods and techniques, I would attempt to extract the pigmentation. Information could be gathered by this process; however, it actually took the fresh hide from a dead horse to extract the purest pigments in quantities from the dermis tissue. The more I worked on this project as a hobby, the more I became interested in the fascinating subject of a horse's color.

A number of the cowboys in the territory were watching this research because nearly every horseman has a preference in the color of his horses, and very likely without any logical explanation other than he just likes them—dun, bay, grey, or so forth. I would put out the word that I was looking for the hide of a horse a certain color. When range horses were being rounded up either for brandin', weanin,' or breakin' young horses and a horse got a leg broke or killed accidentally, if he was the color I had told somebody about, they'd call me to come and get the hide or in some cases, they would bring it to me.

For several years I gathered horse-color specimens and isolated the pigments in my laboratory and made very extensive explanatory notes about each color and filed this information. There are reasons now that I am glad I did this work, even though it was time-consuming and to a degree expensive because there never again will be the assortment of colors or the opportunity to gather the hides of horses for a research project on this subject, and I have in my files the extracted knowledge from the hair, hide, mane, and tail of over one hundred head of horses.

I had gone over close to El Dorado late one afternoon to get the hide of a rare-colored horse that a cowboy had called me about. They had roped this horse in a corral and when he reared and fell to the ground, he fell with his head under his neck and his body lunged forward and broke his neck. It was late when I drove away from the ranch so I spent the night in El Dorado.

I woke up a little before daylight, which was my habit, so I could get back to my practice in the early hours of the morning. I thought I would eat breakfast before I left town so I drove over to Royster's Café. Old Royster ran a good country café, and of course in the ranch country the name Royster had been revised, and he was commonly referred to as Raw Oyster.

Raw Oyster was a good kind of a fellow past middle age whose voice was very broken and rattly and sounded older than he really was. I sat down at the counter and there was only one other customer there at this early hour. Raw Oyster and I had our morning greeting and he told me what little news there was about friends of mine and his that had happened since I was there last. Then in his cracky voice he asked, "What's you gonna eat, Doc?"

"Ham and eggs. I don't guess you've got anything else."

As he wiped his hands on his apron he said, "I've got a few other things like that feller's eatin' over there."

I glanced at the other customer's plate and he had it about cleaned up, so I couldn't tell what else Raw Oyster was serving that morning for breakfast. About that time this fellow got up and left. Raw Oyster turned to his grill and put my breakfast on to cook and started tellin' me about his first customer.

"That feller came in here as soon as I turned on the lights. I set him out a glass of water and as I poured 'im a cup of coffee, I asked 'im, 'What's it for ya?'

"He said, 'I don't know. What you got?'

"Now, Doc, you know that a country café ain't got nothin' but bacon and eggs and ham and eggs and sausage and eggs and cereals and hot cakes for breakfast, so I set in and named all that stuff and it never looked like that I caused him to have no pangs of hunger, so then I said, 'Hot cakes stripped with bacon.'

"His eyes never changed so then I said, 'Hot cakes stripped with ham,' and that never seemed to arouse his taste buds none, and I just thought how ridiculous it would be and I said, 'Hot cakes stripped with chili,' and I'll be damned if he didn't order it and I had to heat up the chili. You heerd me when he offered to pay me and I told him that I'd been tryin' to sell that order for thirty years and he was the first damn fool that ever had nerve enough to try to eat it and he never owed me nothin'."

DROUTH

It hadn't rained in almost a year and a few of the less hardy, who were mostly newcomers, had begun to talk about drouth. It was the custom of the natives to ignore dry weather as long as they possibly could. The old-timers hesitated to start using the word "drouth." They seemed to have some superstitious feelings about admitting that a drouth was in progress, because they seemed to think that when they admitted it, it might make it get worse.

My practice had fallen off a whole lot during this time for many reasons. The first one was that the ranch country still had some old dead grass and other favorable forage that stock were living on and there hadn't been enough rain to cause the poisonous weeds to be in abundance. However, there had begun to be some cases of sheep and cattle eating desert plants that were never intended for animal consumption.

When a flock of ewes are all bred, it is the custom among sheep ranchers to keep the bucks in a pasture to themselves most of the year. The reason for this is so that all the lambs will be the same size and age when they are weighed and shipped in the fall.

Ranchers had begun to ask me in casual conversation about their bucks getting poor. Eventually they would begin to die without any apparent disease, even though they were being fed at least enough feed to live on. However, the condition had developed so slowly that I had not had any calls to treat bucks that were so affected.

Dow Puckett came in one day and said he believed that all his bucks in the Red House trap were affected by something. Every few days he would find one dead, and he wished I would go out and see what could be done.

The Red House trap was at the edge of town just beyond the stock pens. It was a small pasture of one or two sections, and it was no trouble to drive along the pasture roads until I found the bucks. Then I got out and watched them graze. There was little or no grass or weeds on the ground and the common expression was that everything was grazin' with its "head up," which meant that the only feed stuff left was the leaves of low-growing brush. I walked through these bucks and followed them and watched them go from bush to bush and they were gathering little gummy balls of seed from black brush. This was about the only thing they were eating except for the feed they were being given in troughs near the windmill.

I stripped off some of these pods of gummy seed by hand, and, in fact, ate a little of the stuff to see if I could tell why a sheep liked it. By now I had eaten so many desert plants that appealed to sheep that I nearly knew a buck sheep's taste. This stuff had a sweet astringent taste and I really didn't see how it would be detrimental for a sheep to eat it.

When I got through working this waxy seed in my laboratory, I had extracted a substance that was coating the inside of the intestinal tract and shrinking the mucous membranes that absorb the digested nutriments of the sheep's diet. Actually what the sheep were gathering to eat from the black brush was starving them to death.

This was valuable information that I spread among the ranchers without charge so that they would take their bucks off of black brush pastures. I didn't mind passing out the advice because I had no medical treatment for the condition.

Bill McKenzie came by the office early in the morning and said his only milk cow at his ranch near Bakersfield had been sick for several days and had fallen off in her milk production, and they had quit saving the milk until they found what was the matter with her. He wanted me to come on out that day to see the cow, and I told him I had a call at McCamey and I would drop back by his place at Bakersfield a little after noon.

When I drove up to the ranch, Bill had a good Jersey cow in the corral that had a blistered nose from fever. Cows have no sweat glands in the skin covering their body and the only place that a cow does sweat is on the bare skin on her nose and mouth. When one is blistered, it is a symptom that she has had high fever.

I examined this cow thoroughly and listened to a high ratio in her heartbeat. I told Bill that she had some kind of serious internal trouble that I could not positively diagnose and I would treat her for fever; however I was unable to find the real cause of trouble. We discussed the possibility of some foreign object in her stomach, which would be impossible to operate for successfully. Bill wasn't dissatisfied with my diagnosis and understood that it was a case that we just didn't know about and promised to let me know when the cow died. I told him I would come out and cut her open without charge in order to satisfy myself about her trouble for my future use.

In a few days, Bill called me late one afternoon and told me the cow had died an hour or so before. I hurried out to the ranch which was thirty-five miles away, and before any decomposition or swelling set in, we did a thorough postmortem on the cow. I found a crooked piece of baling wire jabbed through the intestinal tract and penetrating into one lobe of her lung, and from the presence of pus and blood, it could have been there for several weeks; this was the cause of death.

As I cut into the different parts of the paunch, we began to remove various objects commonly referred to in practice as "hardware." The term "hardware" is applied to cases where, for the lack of minerals and from pure hunger and starvation, a cow will chew on any piece of old metal that she can get in her mouth. There were nine empty rifle cartridge shells, a pocketknife with the blades broken out, half of a three-inch strap hinge, a piece of small chain nine inches long, and a metal tag off of a buggy dated 1891, Troy, Ohio.

There were hundreds of such cases developing over the drouth area. As long as these various objects did not puncture some of the internal organs or did not build up to cause an obstruction, an animal might live out a normal lifetime unless he died from some other cause.

A few days after this, Herman Chandler drove up in front of my office with a real good bay roping horse in his trailer. He told me he had come through Fort Stockton the day before and I was gone. He was so anxious to get something done for this horse that he had hauled him to Midland to a doctor and to Pecos and back by Monahans, and none of them had been able to diagnose the horse's trouble.

I said, "Herman, unload him to where I can see him on the ground."

While he was unloading the horse, he said he hadn't eaten and had drunk very little for about five days, and he was givin' me a speech about him being the best ropin' horse he ever had and he sure hated to lose him. He was a good horse and was drawn as bad as a wolf that had been in a three-day chase in a snow storm.

After looking at him carefully, I tried to open his mouth and he began to fight his head and run backward. I asked if anybody in examining the horse had ever looked in his mouth.

He said, "Hell, no, and I hadn't thought of that either."

We let him out in a vacant lot in front of my office and got some soft rope to use to pull his hind legs under him and and then tied all four legs together as gently as we could. We took the halter off and fitted a speculum in his mouth and buckled the straps to hold it in place up around the top of his head like the headstall of a bridle.

A horse mouth speculum has ratchets on the side and as it is worked open, it holds the horse's jaws apart to keep him from being able to bite when you go inside of his mouth. His mouth was dry with a thick heavy slime instead of saliva and his breath had an extremely bad odor as he struggled to get up or close his mouth.

Chandler got down on the ground and cradled the horse's head up in his lap and held his nose high for me to put my hand and arm down in his mouth and into his throat. I felt the stub end of something and when I touched it, the horse went into a struggle and moaned like he was in great pain. I came back out of his mouth and got a long pair of heavy-duty forceps and went back and got a hold of this strange object. It took all of Chandler's strength to hold his head as I pulled. When I jerked it out as fast as possible, I had about a five-foot length of sotol blade with little sharp daggers that grew out on each side about a half inch apart and were turned pointed down, which caused them to be imbedded in the horse's throat about the length of the entire blade.

We got the riggin' off his head and untied his feet and let him up. By this time we had a small gathering of ranch people that had noticed the commotion and had walked down to see what was going on. We led the horse back to the office, and I carried water out of the office in a two-gallon bucket until he had drunk about two tubs full. I told Chandler I was afraid to give the horse any more water now and told him to load the animal and take him home; no further treatment would be necessary.

This horse was another case of trying to survive in a drouth by eating desert plants.

I was sittin' on my porch at Stud Flat (this was the name

the natives had given my office when I moved out on Spring Drive on the edge of town) watchin' the heat waves in the middle of the afternoon irradiate from the pebble-rock-covered desert when Abe Mitchell drove up, got out and came in. I said, "Abe, drag up a chair and be slow to bring up your troubles 'cause it's awful damn hot, and I don't much want to make a call until the cool of the evenin'."

We sat there awhile and wiped sweat, and I finally got up and went to the icebox and got us some cold drinks. Soon he began to unload a small amount of his troubles. He said he had a hundred and eighty white-faced cattle, that some of them were about to go blind and all of their eyes were runnin' and looked irritated and sore.

I said, "Abe, I imagine it's the pinkeye."

"I know it is, but how are you goin' to unpink a white-faced cow's eyes and skin?"

We talked on and discussed the various unsuccessful ways that had been tried since the dust had gotten so bad during the drouth. One of the drouth-type conditions that developed first in range cattle was what's commonly referred to as pinkeye. This is a common name for keratitis. There are three types of pinkeye. One is caused by a lack of green feed that occurs in livestock that are kept in barns in northern climates. Another type is actually a bloodstream infection. But the one occurring in the Trans-Pecos Region in my practice was caused by dust, wind, and hot sunshine that irritated the eyes of all breeds of animals. However, pinkeye was not considered common to anything but sheep and cattle.

I told Abe that being a smart doctor, I knew how to unpink the skin and eyes of a white-faced cow and, at the same time, treat the infection.

He said, "I'll have the cattle in the corral early in the morning and I've got a good chute and plenty of help, and if you would get up and tend to business as early in the morning as I'm goin' to, we'll get through treating the cattle before the heat of the day."

Later in the afternoon, I compounded five gallons of saline sulfa solution and added enough methylene blue medical dye to make a real dark-blue solution.

I was at the corral early the next morning as Abe and his cowboys brought the cattle into the corral. The working chute was long enough to hold about twenty-five or thirty head at a time, and the chute had a head squeeze on the gate. We would let a cow stick her head up into the gate and drop a lever down that would catch her head so she couldn't get out but would be able to turn it from one side to the other so that we could treat each eye.

I had a six-ounce drench gun that I filled. As I squirted this solution into the cow's eye with one hand, and as it gushed out, I would catch it with my other hand and smear it all over the white hair and the pink skin of the white-faced cow, which would dye the whole area a dark blue that would stay a week or ten days under range conditions and during that time deflect the sunrays that were causing the irritation of the eye socket itself.

Some of these cows' eyes were so bad that there was already a white scum growth over the eyeball and a few were blind in one eye and one or two were blind in both eyes and followed the rest of the herd around by sound and smell. There was one cow that you could tell was pretty old by the wrinkles on her horns and around her eyes and she had already lost one eye. I gave her a very thorough treatment and when we let her head loose and let her come out of the chute, she turned and refused to leave. When I slapped her on the shoulder and hollered at her, she turned her good eye back up to me for more treatment.

This ten or fifteen days' relief at the most for pinkeye at normal range conditions would have remedied the problem. However, in a drouth that hung on, this was only temporary relief and treatment had to be repeated regularly.

After we turned the cattle out, we watched them stand around in the shade at the water trough, and Abe said, "To see them not rubbin' their heads against one another and to notice the flies gone from around their faces is satisfaction enough for me for the trouble."

With all this evidence of drouth developing in my practice by the middle of 1947, it was hardly possible to continue to ignore dry weather. The small irrigation valley north of Fort Stockton that got its water from the historical Comanche Springs was such a small body of land that it did not begin to produce a fraction of the amount of feed necessary for the great drouth-stricken ranching area. The few pump farms that were being irrigated by wells were of no particular importance in the supply of feed and the depth of water in these wells was dropping by the day.

Dry feed that was being hauled and shipped in for hundreds of miles was a poor substitute for the lush growth of spring and summer weeds or cured mesquite and grama grass for fall and winter grazing. By now, nearly all the ranchers for about a year had been feeding hay as well as some stronger supplementary feed, and as these small ranchers used up their borrowing power, they began to go out of business. Some of the larger ranchers had begun to lease ranches in other parts of the country that were not affected by the drouth.

It was during the following year that many West Texans transplanted themselves to the Arkansas-Missouri grass country to the east and north and the hardier and larger operators moved into Colorado, Wyoming, and Montana.

Those that went to Colorado bettered themselves only for a short season or so because the drouth was spreading that direction.

I still had a practice that afforded some relief from the drouth and I even began to hate cats and dogs and the people that owned them a little less. When Mrs. John Lancaster called me in the middle of a hot day in July to deliver some pigs, I almost welcomed the change.

Mrs. Lancaster lived in the irrigated valley north of town. John was in the oil-field-supply business and was gone from home a lot of the time. They weren't really stock people to begin with; however, they had bought this farm and were raising, among other things, some hogs. She had called to tell me that one of their big hogs was trying to have some little hogs, and she didn't think that the old sow was going to be able to have them and could I come right out.

I got there real quick and the sow had just that minute died from being overfat and gettin' too hot tryin' to have her pigs. Mrs. Lancaster was just sick about the whole deal, but when I put my hand on the sow, I realized the pigs were still alive.

As I did a Caesarean, I told her we might save the pigs if we didn't waste any time. She just thought that would be marvelous and had never heard of such a thing; but if we could save them she would raise them on the bottle. By the time I handed her the first one, she had gotten some big beautiful bath towels, any one of which was worth more than the pigs. As I handed her four of them, she wiped the little things off. While they wiggled and squealed, she just beamed; she was tickled pink to be the mother of four little pigs.

Then she asked, "What can I put them in where they will be clean and cool?"

There wasn't a clean place outdoors nor a cool one, and

in a reckless tone of voice I said, "Why don't you put them in the bathtub"—not thinkin' that she would put them there. But she did take the pigs into the house and put them in a deep bathtub, where the little things couldn't crawl out!

She fed them on a bottle, and I think bathed them as often as she did the children and raised four of the cutest squealing little pigs you ever saw. They were pets and were the most spoiled things that were ever in or around a house, but were in the house more than out. Of course, the trouble with pet pigs is that they grow up to be hogs, and the thought of eating one of the little dears was entirely out of the question. She hired a man with a pickup to come and get them when she was gone, so the parting wouldn't be too painful, and she sent them to a boys' ranch where she just knew they would have a good home.

A stock farmer from up on Pecos River east of Imperial came into my office one day and described the condition of a small herd of cattle—some were sick and others weren't doin' too good.

He was a fellow for whom I had done lots of practice, and without going to look at his cattle, I told him from his description his cattle had been drinking crude oil out of a slush pit that some oil company had failed to fence in. The cattle that had gotten the biggest amount of it would eventually die, I said, and some of the others would recover, but it would be slow and he would have a bunch of poor cattle on hand for a year or so.

I explained to him that if he wanted to have a case against the oil company that I would have to go and do a post-mortem on a cow and firm up the evidence so that I could help him collect damages from the oil company. We discussed this and he said it was a slow process to get damage money out of an oil company that had your land

leased and he believed that the short way would be to
sell 'em.

I said, "Well, I would send them to San Angelo or Midland to one of the stockyards and get them out of the
country."

He didn't commit himself as to how he intended to sell
them, and I didn't charge him anything for the advice because I had actually done no real work on the case. At the
time I supposed that that would be the end of it.

Several days later Charlie Baker, who was sheriff of
Pecos County and bought and sold cattle on the side, came
to me and said that he had a bunch of cattle that he had
bought so cheap that he felt like he stole them. Being the
sheriff he ought to be ashamed of a deal like this, but he
said it was a grown man that sold them and took his
money, so he guessed it was all right, but the cattle weren't
real good and he thought maybe they needed some mineral
supplement or maybe they were wormy. He wanted me to
go look at them and see what I thought they ought to have.

I said, "Charlie, I'll be glad to look at the cattle. Where
are they?"

"Well, I bought them from old So-and-so (this happened
to be the man I had advised to sell 'em) and he's lettin' me
keep them in his alfalfa field since he's already got his last
cutting for the year until I find a place to put 'em."

I was practicing medicine. I wasn't referee'n cow deals,
and I was in no position to divulge what information I already had, so I told Charlie that I would meet him at the
field right after noon that day and we would look at the
cattle. There were twenty-eight head of these cows and
yearlings and they were good-quality Hereford cattle as
far as breeding was concerned, and the ages of the cows
were good, but every cow and every yearling showed
marked signs of having drunk oil.

I had to tell Sheriff Baker that the bargain he got he needn't feel too guilty about since these cattle would slowly dry up on the bone and a few of them would die and the others would not be thrifty for at least another year.

Charlie turned pale and looked surprised that his good constituent would have sold him these cattle when he surely must have known what was the matter with them. I reminded him when he was tellin' me about the deal, he said that the fellow sellin' the cattle was a grown man and he guessed it was all right. I said, "You know, the fellow buyin' the cattle was a grown man too." He let out a weak laugh as we walked to the car.

On the way to town he told me that he had sold that fellow some cattle that weren't "just right" about a year before this. As we drove along, he got reconciled to the deal and said, "I guess he has evened the score and I don't believe that I'll be mad at him for it."

I said, "Charlie, that's big of you, but you still got the cattle."

"Oh, I'll send them to Midland to the auction and get rid of them."

We stopped at the Stockton Pharmacy and had a drink together and he paid me for my call.

In about ten days I got a call from Monahans, Texas, and the man said on the phone that he wanted me to come look at a bunch of sick cattle. Well, this was a common sort of a comment when somebody called me, so I said, "Sure," and told him when I would be there.

It was late afternoon when we drove up to his pasture, and sure enough, there was this same bunch of oil-sick cattle. I was still in no position to let on that I had ever seen the cattle before so I explained to him during a careful examination in his presence what had happened to the cattle. By now the mucous membranes from the inside of the mouth and tongue had begun to sluff off and as we looked into some of their mouths, I explained to him that this same condition was present in the stomach and intestinal tract and that some of these cattle would recover, but most of them were slowly going to die off. I couldn't tell him and wouldn't ask, but I could see as I looked at the cattle that there were already five missing since I had first seen the cattle three weeks prior to this time.

I told him, as I had told the rest of them, that these cattle ought to be shipped to an auction and announced in the ring that they had drunk oil and let the purchaser be aware and pay what he wanted to for them. He agreed with me that that would be the fair thing to do and he would just take his loss and forget about them.

A few days after this, a man called me from Pecos and said that he had bought a bunch of cattle and before he put them on feed, he would like them vaccinated for shipping fever and do whatever was necessary to them that I would suggest so they would get the most good out of the feed he was going to give 'em.

When I got to Pecos, here was the same bunch of cattle with three more missing. I still had no professional right to divulge the history of the cattle, so I went into detail and we caught some of these cattle and looked into their mouths and I explained to him about oil poisoning. He immediately decided that he had better not put them on feed as that would be an expensive way to watch them die. I told him that they should go to a public market with an explanation at the time they were auctioned and sell them for whatever they would bring.

This fellow was a good operator and willing to take his loss rather than to misrepresent the cattle so he sent them back to the livestock market and had the auctioneer announce from the stand that these cattle had drunk crude oil, and he wanted anybody who bid on them to have full knowledge of their condition.

Three days later, a cow trader that was "a wire cutter and a speculator" called me to come and look at some sick cattle that he had pastured close to the Pyote Air Base. He was a pretty sharp old boy and had lied, stole, and cheated until he was fairly well fixed financially. When we drove out to see the cattle, he had them standing next to an oil well with an open slush pit and he told me, "These cattle been poisoned on drinkin' that oil and I've got to sue the oil company so I'm gonna have to have you to testify."

I said, "These cattle drank oil at Imperial, were sold to Fort Stockton, were sold to Monahans, were sold to Pecos, and were sold to you, and you're the only man that has bought them with the understanding that they had previously drunk crude oil, but you are crooked enough to know how to try to make a lot of money out of 'em and when you file your case against the oil company and call me as an expert witness, I'll be able to tell the court (as I pointed to the slush pit) that it was not this oil that poisoned the cattle— and to further add to your overhead, get your checkbook out and pay me thirty-five dollars for this call."

Needless to say, I lost the wire cutter and speculator's practice.

COMMON PRACTICE

Late one afternoon, Mr. Lee called me from Iraan and said that the cowboys had brought the best stud he ever owned into the ranch headquarters, and he was bad sick and had been down on the ground and there were patches of hide gone from various parts of his body where he had rolled against rock and he had beat his head against the ground until his eyes were swollen too, and he asked how soon I could get there. The ranch was seventy-five miles away, and I told him I would be there as soon as I could drive it.

I drove into the ranch just at sundown. The stallion was about fifteen hands high with good conformation, and it was easy to see why Mr. Lee was uneasy about him. I didn't have to examine him very much before I knew that he had a mesquite-bean impaction that would be extremely hard to remove.

Mesquite trees make a long pod that is filled with a sweet sorghum-like-tasting pulp and little oblong hard beans that are high in food value. In the late summer and early fall when mesquite beans begin to ripen, cattle and horses and sheep all will eat them. Sheep have to wait for them to fall on the ground, and at this stage the beans are fairly mature and if they are not eaten will lay on the ground all winter without rotting and are good for feed anytime livestock find them.

Horses and cattle, but especially horses, will pick the beans off the trees after they begin to turn sweet, and as long as there is grass to be eaten along with them, the beans will cause no serious problems and are ideal feed for horses to fatten on. In time of drouth when there is no other green vegeation to be mixed with mesquite beans, horses will eat such enormous quantities of them that they will form an impaction, and a mesquite-bean impaction is real trouble.

As the horse develops fever from this digestive-tract impaction, the fever tends to dry the moisture out of the impaction even more; and as this occurs, the fiber begins to swell, and if some form of treatment isn't given, a mesquite-bean impaction is usually fatal. There are other cases where mesquite beans when eaten, especially by the small pony breed of horses, will cause founder and leave crippling effects after recovery in the feet of the ponies. Flocks of sheep will stiffen from the protein saturation in the tissue around the joints from a solid diet of mesquite beans. All ranchers look forward to a good fall mesquite-bean crop to put the final hardening fat on large livestock before winter.

Mesquite-bean impactions do not respond to the therapeutic action of internal purgative medication, and if over-stimulation of the spasmodic muscles of the intestinal tract is induced by medication, many times the large intestine and colon will rupture and hasten death. The only right way to relieve a mesquite-bean impaction is the hard way, and I mean by that you go into the rectum of a horse with a rubber hose and a pump and a tubful of water and moisten and water the impaction, and after you have stripped off to your waist, reach into the rectum of the horse and actually dig the mesquite bean impaction out with the aid of the water that you are pumping in.

We put this stud in a chute where he couldn't lay down and put bars behind him where he couldn't back up on me and bars in front of him so that he couldn't move about, and by about ten thirty that night I had removed more than a tubful of the bean impaction and had gone far past the colon. Then I started medical treatment.

We saved the stud, and for the next five or six weeks, I had from one to as many calls as I could answer through the day and night for horses that were valuable and could be treated because they were gentle. There were lots of unbroke range horses that could not be treated and many of them died.

There was very little treatment that we could give sheep except to move them to pastures where there were no mesquite trees. Cattle belong to the ruminant family and have more than one stomach, and impactions are rarely if ever a problem. There may be an occasional case of bloat in cattle, but the losses from mesquite beans are minor.

I had just gotten in from one of these mesquite-bean cases and it was late afternoon and I was cleaning up a little in my laboratory when the phone rang. It was a fellow at the Walker oil field about forty miles east of Fort Stockton. He was callin' me about his family milk cow that had calved in the early part of the day, and he said that she was awful sick and thought she had milk fever. This was another one of those hurry-up-type calls because the condition becomes critical so fast that time is important.

In an oil field that is already developed and has settled down to production, there is a class of employees that live in those camps after the boomers have passed on—pretty stable citizens. One or maybe two families keep a good milk cow and furnish fresh milk to the rest of the people in the camp, and these pet milk cows become pretty important.

Only the best milk cows will have milk fever because they deplete their body supply of calcium during the previous milking period. When a new calf is born, nature is partial to producing milk for that baby calf, so that the purest available calcium in the cow's body is contained in the white cartilage walls of the milk glands that come out of the body and go into the cow's bag. When the calcium is robbed from these tubes, they collapse and the disintegration that sets in is referred to as milk fever. It is actually a condition instead of a disease, and the cow is sure to die unless you can hastily replace this calcium.

It was after dark when I got there. This good cow was lying stretched out on the ground almost lifeless and no more than an hour from certain death if she received no treatment. Her breathing and heart ratio were so unstable that I had to spend about fifteen minutes of very precious time with heart stimulants before I dared to slug the jugular vein with calcium gluconate, an excess amount of which would have stopped this cow's weak heart. She responded to the hypodermic heart stimulant, which, of course, also raised her fever but enabled me to administer calcium gluconate intravenously.

As I worked on this cow, I was aware of a very medicine-like odor that I knew I had nothing to do with, so I asked what it was that I smelled on the cow. It was late October and by this time of night the onlookers had built a fire in the corner of the corral and the neighbor women had gathered to see what was goin' on and worry about the cow and get in a little gossipin'. When I asked what I smelled on the cow, one of these good neighbor women spoke up and said she bathed the cow's bag with Watkin's Liniment.

After a good forty-five minutes of hard medical practice, the cow showed a very favorable reaction and the men and me took her by the legs and rolled her over on the other side to encourage circulation on the side she had been lying on. She got a tremendous reaction from the calcium and started tryin' to get up.

Well, being a pet cow she was easy to help, and we got her on her feet. She stood there for a few minutes, gained her balance, and walked over to the water trough and drank a lot of water, which was the natural thing for a cow to do that had just started to develop a tremendous flow of milk and had also been dehydrated by temperature.

I leaned back against the fence, and as the cow bawled for her baby calf, I had a real good feeling from saving that fine milk cow. About that time the old lady that had furnished the liniment flipped her apron up and wrapped both hands in it as she passed me goin' toward the corral gate and in a very firm voice said, "Well, we'll never know whether it was the liniment or the doctor that done it!"

About daylight one fresh fall morning, I went out to the irrigation valley north of town to see some sheep that had bloated in the night while grazing on some fresh cut-over alfalfa stubble. This was a common occurrence and the treatment was simple, but the cause was interesting in that it was not covered by any source of veterinary literature and was gradually learned by me and the farmers in the irrigated valley.

In the early fall when the days are still warm in the desert and the nights get very cold along after midnight, sheep will graze and fill up and lay down on dark nights and it's likely that they may not leave their bed until sunrise the next morning. However, when the moon comes up late after the chill of the night, this sudden change from warm days to cold nights causes a chemical reaction in the tender growth of alfalfa and the sugars of the plant turn to acid and are not transposed again until up in the morning hours of warm sunshine.

During this moonlight period of acid vegetation, sheep will come off their bed ground in the moonlight and graze the alfalfa and develop severe cases of bloat within the matter of a few hours. Most of the farmers grazing alfalfa late in the year learned to pen their sheep on dry feed during the moonlight nights and this prevented those early daylight calls for bloat.

I heard a young veterinary doctor had moved in over at Monahans, which was about fifty miles north of me, and I just thought to myself that if he was real good, I would be glad for him to have the north end of my territory up and down the Pecos River, which would better enable me to take care of the rest of my practice.

I had answered a call up to Kermit still further north than Monahans and was on my way home in the late afternoon and dropped by to get acquainted with the young doctor. He was a great big, fat, slick-faced kid fresh out of college who had been raised on pavement and had no livestock or agricultural background. I was as polite to him as I could be and welcomed him into the country and told him I would be glad to help him any way I could and would be sure to send him some practice. As I drove away, I was sure that the only practice I could send him that he would know anything about would be dogs and cats and the women that owned them.

In about three weeks after meeting him, I got a call to come to Monahans to see about a milk cow. I told the people on the phone that they had a young veterinary doctor there and it would be cheaper for them to have him than for me to make the trip. The old man spoke up and said, "We've had him five times and don't think the cow wants him any more, and for what he charges and what we've heard about you, you'd be the cheapest by a whole lot."

About an hour and a half after that, I drove into the side gate of the man's house in the main part of Monahans and there stood his milk cow with one side of her head swelled out of all proportion. He explained to me that the young doctor had used some great long words tellin' him what was the matter with the cow. He said that the words hadn't helped him none and the shots he had been givin' hadn't helped the cow none, and he guessed it wasn't a common case as what was usually referred to as lump jaw.

Lump jaw is caused by an iodine deficiency and the jaw bone becomes porous and the flesh around the bone becomes highly irritated and the swelling usually appears on one side of the head. I looked at this old cow a few minutes and she was in real pain and was standing with her mouth open. Her mouth had been open so much and so long that the end of her tongue was dry and sore.

She was a gentle cow, so we didn't put a rope or anything on her. I just walked up and talked to her a few minutes and reached in her mouth and took hold of her tongue and pulled it out to one side of her mouth. The reason for this is that a cow or horse can't close their mouth to bite your arm if you have it blocked open by having their own tongue pulled out to one side.

As I examined her jaw teeth with one hand, I ran on to something that didn't belong in a cow's mouth. I went to my car and got a long blunt screwdriver and after pulling her tongue out the same way, I went back in her mouth and began to prize on something in line with the teeth in the lower jaw. In a matter of seconds out of her mouth popped a golf ball that had been wedged between two teeth in a socket where a tooth was gone. There had been a mass of feed compressed down into the socket under the golf ball, and, of course, the pus began to flow and the jaw began to go down.

There was a garden hose handy that was hooked to a hydrant so we turned it on and ran cold water through that old gal's mouth for about ten minutes. After I stuck the hose in her mouth and the water started running through her jaw, I turned her tongue loose and she stood with her mouth open and enjoyed the relief she was gettin' from the water washing out all that foreign matter. When I quit runnin' the water, she walked over to the feed trough and began to eat like she was about to starve to death.

This gave me kind of a sickening feeling for the profession when doctors were being turned out of school that didn't have common sense or nerve enough to stick their hand in a cow's mouth to see what was the matter.

The winters in the Southwestern deserts are the most enjoyable time of the year. There are cold nights and warm, still days and just occasional unpleasant spells of weather. During this time of year, the ranchers weren't too busy and most of them took time to have their horses' teeth looked after. It was also an ideal time to do surgery on horses and cattle because there was practically no airborne infections and most recoveries were uneventful.

I had been doing lots of dentistry on saddle horses and that caused talk around the coffee gathering and everybody went to thinkin' about their horses. On one of these nice, clear, cold January mornings, we were sittin' in the drugstore waitin' for the sun to come up so we could shed our coats and enjoy the desert climate when John Vic came up to me and in his high, whiny voice asked me what ought to be done about blind teeth on a four-year-old horse.

I explained to him that we could take the baby teeth out where the permanent teeth could come on through, but that the big knots that had formed on the horse's head over the teeth would not go down after the baby teeth had been pulled and those knots would always show. So we made arrangements for me to remove the baby teeth.

Within a few days, Charlie Dees called me to look at a grey three-year-old colt that he had gotten from the Allison Ranch. This colt had been stifled (stifle joint dislocated), and I explained to Mr. Dees that there was nothing that could be done for this horse and that he would never be any better.

John Bennett came in within a day or two. He had a four-year-old dun horse that was known to be mean to buck and had a white spot in his eye, and he wanted to know if I could do something to cause the spot to disappear. I gave him some powder to be blown into the horse's eye every other day and said, "If anything will take the spot off, this medicine will."

In a few days John Vic came to me and told me that he had traded the horse that I had worked on his teeth for the stifled horse that Mr. Dees had and that Mr. Dees had told him that I said that the leg would get well.

Several days later, Charlie Dees, who was a little old man who wore a smile and a hearing aid and had one leg a little shorter than the other from some injury in his youth that caused him to pace a little when he walked, came up to me on the street. He told me that he had traded the horse he got from John Vic to John Bennett for a horse that had a little spot in his eye. Mr. Bennett had told him that I said the spot would go away, and he just wanted to ask me how long did I think it would take before it would be gone.

I said, "Yeah, and John Bennett said that I had told John Vic that the knots on the horse's head would go away. Now, John Vic lied about the knots goin' away, John Bennett lied about me sayin' that the spot would go out of the horse's eye, and if you told John Vic that the horse's leg that you traded him would get well, or if you told John Bennett that I said the knots would go away, you lied, too—of course, you know whether you said it or not."

As I finished my remark, he turned and started pacing off as though he didn't hear me and said, "Aw wal, didn't matta'."

One hot summer day about noon I got a call from Roswell, New Mexico, concerning some cattle that were dying in the feed lots. The man calling gave me a lot of information about how many different kinds of "shots" they had given these cattle, but they were still dying, though they didn't have any apparent sickness.

I told him there were several good veterinarians closer to him than me, and he said that he didn't know about that because he had tried the most of 'em, and he and some other feed-lot operators had decided that they needed some outside help. He went on to tell me that they had heard that I "worked" on poisons and they would be willing to pay me to come up and look at their troubles. It was about two hundred and twenty miles to Roswell, and I told him I would be there before dark.

There were several of these big feed lots around Roswell, and they were being operated very efficiently, business-wise, and were using the best of milling and mixing equipment in making their feed-lot rations. There weren't any sick cattle out of about three thousand that they showed me from the time I got there till midnight, but I did note there would be an occasional steer that did not appear to be carrying as much fill as the rest of the cattle.

I went to the old Nickson Hotel and checked in and told the several fellows that had taken me over the feed lots that I would see them at breakfast. This was another case of needin' to be a better detective than doctor, and I decided to go to sleep and forget about it all till morning.

I spent the next day in the feed lots south of town trying to find some source of chemical poison that might be getting into the feed through the milling process. Late in the afternoon three steers died within an hour of each other, and these were cattle I had seen the day before that hadn't shown any signs of illness.

I hadn't been wishin' for a steer to die, but this was sure enough a start because I could "post" them and possibly pick up some indication of the trouble from the internal organs. The steers that had died were two years old and had been on feed long enough to show bloom but weren't quite fat enough to be termed finished. There was no indication of anything wrong in the liver, spleen, or kidneys, which are the organs that first show damage or presence of poison.

We went back to the office at one of the feed lots a little after dark and sat and talked for about three hours, and I told these feeders that their outside help up to now hadn't found anything seriously wrong.

Early the next morning while it was still cool, I was sittin' on the curb in front of the Nickson Hotel with Frank Young, waitin' for the feeders. Frank was an old-time sheriff and had been head of the State Police of New Mexico, but since his retirement from political life, he was in the real estate business with an office in the hotel.

We were looking out across the courthouse lawn when a middle-aged man started walking across the lawn on feet big enough for a man twice his size, long arms and hands that hung down almost to his knees, and his head was shaped about as round as a hicker nut.

Frank said, "You see that fellow goin' yonder?"

He was the only one crossing the lawn and I said, "Yeah, what about him?"

"That's the most ignorant man in the world."

"Aw, Frank, I don't see much difference in the way he looks and a bunch of the other natives around here."

Frank was a big, dark-complexioned fellow, and when he laughed his belly jumped up and down. He laughed real big and said, "I don't care, there's some difference."

"What's he done that makes you think that he's the champion of ignorance?"

"Well, there was a big family of them people living back up in the mountains. They made their livin' by hard labor, cuttin' posts and trappin' varmints, but the youngest one saved his money and got a hold of some good teams, wagons, harnesses and other equipment, and he left here and got jobs doin' dirt work on railroad right-of-ways.

"He wanted to come home and visit a few days and he decided he would send a wire and gave it plenty of time to be delivered, so some of his family could come in and meet him at the train. When the depot agent got the wire, he stuck it in his pocket and walked up here on the square, and that one you see goin' yonder was loafin' over by the saloon.

"The depot agent walked up and said, 'Rufe, I've got a wire here from your brother, Eck.' Rufe took the wire and looked at it a minute and said, 'Yep, that's Eck all right. I'd've knowed his handwrite anywhere.'"

About that time some of the feeders drove up and we went to the feed lot. I walked around among fat cattle, fresh feed, and hidden trouble looking for symptoms.

These feed-lot operators had started the practice this year of feeding green chopped feed the first thing in the morning fresh out of the field. Corn was planted in the irrigation fields as thick in rows as it could stand, and with liquid fertilizer added to the irrigation water, this corn grew eight to ten feet high real quick. Before the stalk and foliage had time to start getting tough, it was cut and chopped by a machine in front of a truck that was especially equipped with a feed body on it. As this feed was cut green and chopped, it was moved by a conveyor over the cab of the truck and into this specially built body as the chopping machine and truck moved down the rows of feed. Then this truckload of fresh green chopped feed was hauled up to the feed lot and a specially built auger filled the troughs from the side of the body as the truck drove down the alleys between the different feed lots.

Fresh green chopped feed going through this process

could have some chemical reactions occur between the time it was chopped in the field and the matter of four or five hours before the cattle would finish eating it all. I rode the truck in the field and watched the chopping going on, and then I walked around through the feed lots all morning watching the steers eat this green feed before they were given their mixture of concentrated dry feeds that after-noon.

The green chopped feed grown under irrigation was juicy and good and had a nice smell when piled up in the trough, and the steers like it. Late that afternoon I took a saddle horse and rode down through the corn for no particular reason that I can give, other than riding around on a good horse through green fields was at least restful and the company of a good horse sometimes improved my thinkin'.

As I was unsaddling the horse about dark, one of the men working around the feed lot had come back to the feed mill to tell me that he saw a steer dying in the last pen as he had started home. I got in my car and drove down close where I would have my instruments and other supplies with me and this fellow stayed and helped me post the steer.

This time I was looking harder and thought I'd better do a very thorough job if I were going to find the trouble. I took the paunch, which has separating divisions in it—and it's generally stated that a cow has three or four stomachs, depending on what you are going to term a stomach, and this assembly constitutes the paunch—and washed all the waste matter and undigested feed out with a hose. As the pressure of the water hit the lining of the stomach, the lining would sluff off and after it dried was brown and had the same thickness and feel as a piece of printing parchment. I had found the trouble—but what caused it?

I carefully cleaned the rest of this paunch without an

more water and stuffed it into some large glass jars that I had in the back of my car and tightly sealed the lid on them. It would be necessary for me to go back to my home laboratory with these specimens to do a good job of analyzing and diagnosing.

I called the hotel from the feed lot and told them that I was leaving but not to check me out and to tell whoever might be lookin' for me that I would be back the next night. I reached Fort Stockton by midnight and by morning I had ground this fresh paunch, extracted all the serum and juices with the addition of triple-distilled water, and through a distillation process had about four liquid ounces of a very potent chemical insecticide. Now the problem was, Where did it come from? I had not been able to find it in any of the feeds that I had analyzed.

I drove into Roswell in the early afternoon and told the feed-lot operators of my discovery. We started hunting for an agricultural chemical insecticide. I finally wound up back in the cornfield, and in the hot, bright sunshine, I got a glimmer of a strange lacquer-looking finish over the leaves and some of the stalks of the corn.

I cut about twenty stalks of corn and headed back for my laboratory, and after a careful washing and distillation process, I was headed back to Roswell two days later with the same chemical substance in a vial that had been extracted from the lining of the steer's paunch.

When I told the feed-lot operators this, they all said that they were spraying the lush tender corn with an insecticide in an oil base that they had been assured was harmless. The very explicit guaranteed instructions on the container stated that this insecticide would be harmless to livestock to graze the vegetation after three weeks from the time it was applied.

The extracted chemical from the steer's paunch was sufficient evidence to call the chemical company in on the case. I put in a long-distance call to Michigan, and they assured me that extensive research had been done and that my diagnosis could not be possible. The next morning a staff of scientists landed at the airfield and came to the hotel with the positive intention of having my scalp, professionally speakin', in the matter of a short time.

I had investigated the area where they had done their experimentation as best I could from a distance. All of their experiments had been conducted in acid soils with natural rainfall of more than forty inches per year, and with the usual amount of dew and fog at night that would occur in climates of this humid nature, leaching and dissipation of chemicals from the foliage would occur and it was true that such vegetation would be clear of any chemical residue in three weeks.

The desert regions of New Mexico had little or no summer rainfall, hardly any dew, and never any fog, and there was no dissipation of a chemical substance in an oil base sprayed onto lush corn, and the heat of the desert sun caused it to dry suddenly and be firmly fixed to the foliage of the corn.

I ran back and forth between Roswell and my laboratory at Fort Stockton three or four times during the next several days and came up with much proof and evidence. The president of the company had flown in on the case, and he was a high-class business executive who was concerned with the facts, and if his company was liable, he was interested in a peaceful settlement without publicity.

However, their chemist, so far as my judgment of stock was concerned, was a little on the stupid side. His hairline in front nearly touched his eyebrows and there was a ridge across the front of his head that showed his skull was as thick as my thumb, and whatever he knew he had left at home in his test tubes. Of course, he was in a hot spot and was determined to shed as much bad light on me as possible.

At a meeting of all concerned parties back at the hotel, I had with me three separate 4-cc. vials of chemicals that I had very carefully filtered under exact conditions. I took them out of my pocket in the midst of a conversation after Mr. Chemist Wizard had gotten unpleasant and set them on the desk and told him that with his vast knowledge and acute observation that I was sure he would be able to tell which of these three vials had its content drawn from a fresh-opened container of the chemical, which had been distilled from the tissue of the steer's paunch, and I was sure he would have no trouble knowing which vial had been gathered and distilled from the green corn.

He stood and looked at the vials a few minutes and sweat broke out on his forehead, and he wet his lips and wiped his head with a white handkerchief. By now the president of the company wasn't too proud of him and didn't think that he was goin' to win any blue ribbons anyway, so he insisted that he identify where the substance in each of the vials came from.

I had numbered the vials and written on a piece of paper their identity and had given it to Frank Young, who was a disinterested party, to keep until the proper time. Frank was sittin' in a chair over in the corner of the room and I think he had begun to wonder whether my luck would hold or not.

After considerable hesitation, this expert of experts identified the pure sample as the one off the corn, and the sample from the steer's stomach to have come out of the container, which left the third sample to have come out of the steer's stomach, which was wrong too.

I told Frank to hand Mr. President my note, and as he finished reading it to himself, he turned to his secretary and said, "Pay all just claims as represented, and be sure to pay the doctor his fee and expenses."

YELLOWWEED
FEVER

In late November of my second year in Fort Stockton, yellowweed was lush and had enough size that I could begin to pull it and continue the experiment I had started my first winter but had been halted by the tough summer weed. I had started to go pull some yellowweed to feed the experimental sheep when an old man stopped me as I was gettin' in my car. He happened to be one member of the welcoming committee that had told me the country didn't need me when I arrived. He said he had a bull that was damn bad sick and for me to hurry up and follow him out to his ranch in my car. I said, "Surely you must be mistaken."

He looked at me hard and bellowed out that he wasn't no doctor, but he had enough sense to know when a bull was sick.

I said, "Well, it don't seem possible when you told me that this was a healthy stock country. Besides that, I don't believe that I can be worried about him because you told me that when there was a 'die-out' here, there was always enough left to restock the country."

This made the old man holler and wave both hands and he told me that he didn't want to lose no bull just because of some bull he put out once, and he would consider it a favor if I would come and doctor his bull.

I asked him, "Well, you sure that you want to spend money to have me doctor stock for you when you could do it just as good yourself?"

This would have made him mad only he was pleading by now and said, "I've done doctored the bull and he ain't no better."

For meanness, I said, "Do you suppose I've got to cure what's the matter with him and what you done to him too?"

In desperation he said, "Hell, you can charge me double. Let's go doctor the bull!"

The bull got all right after I treated him and the old hardhead may never have bragged on me but he, at least, shut up talkin' about the country not needin' me.

In the summer I had done a great deal of research on the therapeutic action of drugs that would be usable in feeds that I hoped would counteract the toxic effect of vegetation that grew in an alkali soil. By now, this research had begun to get expensive and it had taken a lot of the money I had earned in my general practice to carry on this project. However, sheep were more plentiful than money and I had no trouble getting plenty furnished me by those who were hopeful that the research would be successful.

The first sheep that I was feeding this second winter on still another formula died the sixteenth day from the beginning of the test, which was five days longer than one had lived up to this time. The last sheep to die in this group lived thirty-four days. This was the first sign of improvement since I had started working on the project about a year before, and this was the twenty-seventh medical preparation I had tried.

It had still been impossible for me to break the liquid of the fiber and extract anything harmful from the contents; however, I continued to grind weed and work with it, and the back of my office had a sickening sweet, fresh yellowweed smell that filled the air for months and months.

With the encouragement from the last group of sheep, I reworked that particular formula and started on another group of four sheep. In this group there was one half-breed Navaho sheep. He was older than the others and bigger and ate more weed than any of the other sheep. I pulled weed nearly all winter for this bunch of sheep and the first one died on the forty-third day. The other two died within sixty days, and the big old Navaho sheep got sick but refused to die and I turned him out in the spring.

This particular experiment caused quite a lot of conversation around and more than a few people drove over to the Posse grounds to see these sheep.

I was ready to start feeding sheep the third winter when Dow and I decided that we could have better water and feed arrangements in a corral at the Red House pasture south of the stock pens on the north side of Dow Puckett's ranch. This was a handy place to get to from town and was real close to all the yellowweed that I needed to pull up and down the draw in the same pasture.

I had changed my formula several times by now, using some rabbits and guinea pigs to experiment with. This particular formula was number forty-seven and was the last in a two-year period of experimentation. I had compounded the medical ingredients in my laboratory for all these experiments and this one I mixed into soybean meal and put it in a trough at the rate of one half pound of medicated feed per sheep per day.

Drugs cannot be used in a dry-feed mixture successfully unless they are all in fine powder form. Any variety of ground grain is included to let the drug elements sift to the bottom of the trough and will not afford a uniform dose of medication in the feed. However, heavy protein meals, such as cottonseed and soybean meal, are finely ground and are much heavier and still contain a small percentage of oils and this makes it possible to mix powdered drugs with meals into a stable proportion that will be reasonably equally mixed in the trough as the feed is eaten, thereby ensuring a uniform dose of medication.

I still had help from some of the ranchers around, and the days that I was too busy I would see them at coffee or pass them on the road and tell them that I needed weed for the sheep and 'most everyone was glad to help. When someone passing by saw them pulling weed, they'd hurrah 'em about Doc Green havin' them on yellowweed too.

All four of these experimental sheep lived and thrived on a complete diet of yellowweed with the supplemental half pound of medicated feed. However, the yellowweed year was over and the big pasture demonstration experiment remained to be tried the coming fall and winter.

By now there were a good many ranchers who thought the research and formula showed promise and were very enthusiastic about the possibility of grazing yellowweed successfully. However, there were still a lot of skeptics who advanced the idea that you might be able to pull weed and keep sheep in a pen and make them live, but it would never be successful to feed in the pasture where sheep could graze their own diet of yellowweed.

Several different methods were used in trying to live with yellowweed and graze sheep on it. Some pastures that were good with the exception of a certain yellowweed-infested hill or ridge could be used by fencing off the yellowweed and leaving that part of the pasture idle. In many cases these fenced-off yellowweed traps might amount to as much as two or three thousand acres.

Another practice followed by ranchers who had pastures that were partially free of yellowweed was to rotate the sheep. Instead of having the proper number of sheep in each pasture, they would concentrate all of them into one yellowweed pasture and let them eat the yellowweed down the ground; with so many sheep none of them would get enough to make them sick, and this took about three days. Then the sheep would be scattered back into the regular pasture for a week or so and then all back into the yellowweed pasture. This procedure would go on all winter, which meant lots of ridin', herdin', handlin', and chousin' during the winter months. The theory behind this was that if they ate the weed up for enough years that it wouldn't seed, and some thought that they would kill it out and get rid of it.

There was another practice that was far more expensive and this was used on ranches that had nothing but yellowweed. The sheep would be turned into a yellowweed pasture for several days, and at the first signs of sickness they would be put in a corral on alfalfa hay and fed a full ration until the yellowweed was fed out of them. This was an extremely costly and not too satisfactory method, but it was another way to survive the yellowweed season.

Drugs that I had needed for these limited group experiments had been fairly easy to purchase in the small quantities, but now it was necessary that I arrange for enough drugs to feed seventy-five to one hundred sheep for as long as sixty days or more.

The meal mixtures were far better than grain mixtures, but the final perfection of dosage would have to be accomplished by the pelleting of these mixtures into sheep-size pellets. This brought me to the decision to have the feed for the pasture experiment run through a pellet machine at some feed mill, in order to make sure that each sheep would get its proper dose. When I began to contact the drug companies for these medications and ask for some of them in quantities of a hundred pounds, I discovered that there had never been such an extensive use of any of these elements, and quantity procurements would pose a real problem.

I bought up all the quantity stocks that I could find for my next year's experiment and by early fall had enough medication to process 1,400 pounds of medicated feed. I didn't have equipment and there was no one available in my territory to compound a medical formula for 1,400 pounds of feed, so Dow Puckett and I went out to his ranch headquarters to use a small hand-turned concrete mixer to mix these drugs.

The mixing of this formula in such quantities was going to be a pretty messy job, because the coarse animal charcoal continues to break and give off dust that goes deep into clothes fibers and deeper into skin and under fingernails and works around to the back side of your eyeballs, and so we put on some old clothes and began mixing. As Dow was turning the crank on the mixer and I was breaking up any lumps or clods in the drum with my hand, we were both getting a good coat of charcoal dust and powdered medicine over us and I asked, "Dow, do you feel like you are about to go down in medical history with Dr. Lister and Pasteur?"

Dow laughed real big and said, "I think when this is over

we can go into town disguised as misplaced coal miners and nobody would recognize us."

A few cranks and another coat of dust later he said, "Since I'm turning the crank, I'll be Henry Ford. He made the most money. You be Pasteur."

This kind of conversation kept the day's mixing from turning into real work. It turned out that by the time we had finished sackin' and loadin' the mixture in my car that Dow's description of us was far more accurate than either of us being put into medical history.

Soybean or cottonseed meal was very scarce and at that time of year the new crop of seed had not come in and I was having trouble finding any. H. H. Matthews, superintendent of the El Sinora Cattle Company, operated a three-hundred-section ranch. It was strictly a cow ranch and Mr. Matthews was not interested in sheep, but he was interested in the country and his fellow ranchmen and was glad to see the research being done. I had done some practice for the El Sinora and our business relations had been pleasant.

The El Sinora had two or three tons of soybean meal that by some mistake had been delivered to them with a carload of soybean cake, and Mr. Matthews agreed to sell as much of this meal as I wanted, on the condition that I NOT pay for it with cash but that I had to practice it out on the El Sinora as they needed me. He explained that the El Sinora Cattle Company, whose bookkeeping office was in San Antonio, had no arrangements to buy and sell feed, but it would be all right for me to render statements marked paid for my services until such feed had been worked out.

Several months before this, my friend Gid Reding had built a solid concrete building. One side of the building was partitioned off for my office and there was a partition separating my laboratory from the front office. Gid opened a whisky store on the other side of this new building, and with a whisky store and a horse doctor in the same building, the native cowboys immediately named it THE MEDICAL ARTS.

It was in the front office of the Medical Arts that I moved out the furniture and covered the floor with building paper, pulled off my boots and in my bare feet on the floor mixed and compounded drugs with 1,400 pounds of soybean meal, using a garden rake and a stove shovel. By raking and shoveling it up against one wall and working it back on the floor against the other wall, I was using the same principle of shoveling and raking as would be used by a druggist compounding powders with a spatula.

While I was mixing this feed, Scuddy, the plumber from next door, stopped by, stuck his head in, watched me a minute, and said, "Doc, I'll turn the water on that if you want to make a loblolly while you're playing."

I got a lot of this kind of good-natured native help.

By now it was early fall, and I was anxious to get this feed ready far in advance of the time I would start using it. I naturally assumed that any feed mill would be glad to run this mixture through their pellet machine for me and compress it into one-half-inch sheep-size pellets. Early the next Monday morning I hooked on my horse trailer and loaded this sacked mixture and started to San Angelo, one hundred and sixty-five miles to the cottonseed oil mill.

The manager of the mill thought they could do this little chore for me, but it would be late in the afternoon before there would be a break in the cow-size cottonseed cake that they were running. When they changed to a half-inch die, they would run my pellets for me. I backed up to the dock and unloaded my meal and mixture and planned to spend the day around San Angelo and haul my finished feed back that night.

I went back late that afternoon to discover that the manager didn't have a whole lot to do with running the mill, and the mill superintendent had refused to have anything to do with the stinkin' stuff. So, I loaded it in my trailer and drove to Ballinger, to another cottonseed mill. They listened to my story and said their customers didn't have much yellowweed and were not interested in wasting much time trying to clean up their bins and other equipment after having had that there medicine in it.

By this time I had between three and four years' worth of research invested in this forty-seventh formula and that included many weary nights of laboratory work and lots of hours of pulling yellowweed together and all the post-mortems and so forth, so I wasn't about to be discouraged by being turned down a few times by mill operators.

I drove from Ballinger over to Abilene to a mill owned by the Paymaster Milling Company. The mill was running on a twenty-four-hour shift and it was late in the night, so I curled up in my car and went to sleep to wait for the office staff to show up for work the next morning.

The manager of the mill was there about seven thirty, and I told him my story about all the research and experimentation that had been done on this formula and explained to him the reasons for wanting it made into pellet form. He was just a little short of polite and told me that they were making cow-size cottonseed cake that they knew cattle would eat and was already sold and waiting to be milled and delivered, and he wasn't going to break into that kind of a money-makin' arrangement to mess with some kind of medicated "mix-up." I had had a bad night's rest in my car and hadn't eaten breakfast, and I gave him a fair cussin' and drove off.

I had a few more mild refusals from mixed-feed mills that made grain cubes, and the third day after I left home, I drove back and unhooked the trailerload of feed in front of my office, still not processed, and began to ponder the expense and trouble of having to buy a pellet machine of my own.

This trailerload had been sitting in front of my office for several days when Johnny Clark, a feed salesman for the Minimax Feed Mill in Lamesa, Texas, came by to visit me. Johnny was a very aggressive salesman and was interested in the welfare of his territory and the possibility for a new business. He told me that he would take it up with the management at their mill and call me.

He knew that I left early and rode hard, and the next morning he called me before daylight and told me that he had discussed the matter with Roscoe Holton, the general manager for the Higginbotham interests, who owned the Minimax Mill. John must have done a good job of presenting my case because his instructions were to tell me that they would cooperate to the fullest extent and that I should bring in at my convenience whatever I had that needed milling.

I left the next morning with my load of feed. We unloaded and started milling before noon. It turned out that this was not going to be so simple since the holes on the die of the pellet machine were tapered, and as the feed was pushed in from the inside of the die, the pellet was formed by the feed passing through the tapered hole under pressure. The drugs in the presence of heat and pressure caused the pellets to be much harder. In fact, so much harder that it was doubtful that sheep could eat them.

Johnny, Roscoe, and even the mill foreman worried and discussed this situation and decided to use an old die that had been discarded because the taper had been cut out by too much use. This turned out to be ideal because this minimum amount of taper made a pellet of the right firmness.

We spent all day changing dies and regrinding pellets until we had all the feed in pellet form, and about dark we loaded it on to my trailer. Minimax Mill refused to take any pay for their services, apologized for the delay, and expressed their willingness to continue with whatever I needed to have done. I drove home feeling better about the situation and stored this feed for the yellowweed season.

Rains had been good that summer and I began looking around for a yellowweed pasture that would be free of any desirable vegetation. J. Harrison Dycke had a ranch about six miles north of Fort Stockton and he, Dow Puckett, Doug Adams, Concho Cunningham, Ernie Hamilton, and I drove out and went over most of the ranch and picked out a four-hundred-acre block that in their opinion was the solidest growth of yellowweed on the ranch—or on earth, for that matter.

Harrison had helped me pull yellowweed several times for the other experimental sheep and was glad to cooperate in every way possible to help me to run this pasture test. He fenced off the four-hundred-acre plot from the rest of the ranch. This plot contained one big long water trough where the sheep would have to water, and this would make them easier to observe.

This was range country, about three thousand feet elevation, and this particular pasture was rolling country covered with low-growing, scrubby, black brush and greasewood, with a few mesquite trees in the draws. The only grass in the pasture was tough bunch grass, commonly referred to as burro grass, which sheep seldom eat except in the early summer when tender shoots come out close to the ground. Yellowweed covered all the slopes and the upper end of the draws and grew up to the shade of some catclaw bushes that were on the ridge.

Dow Puckett furnished seventy-five head of cut-back

lambs that were of too small and inferior quality to sell with the usual lamb crop. We took particular pains to tatoo a number in the ear of each one of these sheep in case I needed to keep individual records as to their sickness and recovery. I kept them in a lot a few days to be sure they knew how to eat feed before we put them on the yellowweed pasture.

Range livestock that have been grazed on grass and browse all their life and have never learned to eat domestically produced feeds have to be confined a few days with feed before them in a trough. After they get hungry enough to smell around, a few start eating; then the rest of them will catch on plenty fast. The best way to teach sheep to eat grain or milled feed products such as pellets is to use alfalfa hay and mix the other feed in the trough with it. Since sheep are natural green-feeders, they will take to the alfalfa first and gradually learn to eat the other forms of feed. It is always necessary to know that the sheep are all eating, and if necessary, take out the noneaters before they are put in the pasture on poisonous weeds. Otherwise, they would not be getting their dose of medication with each day's feed.

When I had them switched off alfalfa and they were all eating the medicated pellets, it was time to move them to the yellowweed pasture. The other fellows who were interested and had been helping me with their pickups and trailers helped me haul these sheep by the railroad's stock pen and unload them and weigh them. The average weight of this seventy-five head was 63⅖ pounds. Then we reloaded them and took them out to the yellowweed pasture and unloaded them at the water trough.

Any flock of sheep or other livestock will "walk out" the new pasture that they have been moved to and get acquainted with it the first few days and nights, so the next morning these sheep were well scattered. They hadn't learned to come to call and I rounded them up horseback and brought them close to the water trough and poured the medicated soybean half-inch pellets on the ground. I sat around on my horse and made sure that they all ate feed.

In just a few days these sheep all came to call and were filling up on the lush tender yellowweed and were eating their daily protein supplement with the medicine in it. By the eleventh day everybody who knew about the experiment was looking for some sick sheep. There were no signs of sickness and all the sheep were staying full on fresh yellowweed and all were coming to their daily feed and medication.

By the twentieth day the talk around coffee had begun to take on a different tone and the common remark that "Maybe Doc's found something" sounded good to my ears. However, the diehards and fogies were saying "just give 'em time—they'll get sick 'fore long."

By the thirtieth day no sheep were sick and I began to have visitors go out with me in the mornings when I fed. It was the general opinion of those who had seen the sheep when I first put them out there that they were gaining weight on a solid diet of yellowweed plus the protein and medication. A half pound of protein feed per day will not fatten a sheep but is only a supplementary winter feeding, so this began to focus the attention on the fact that yellowweed was a nutritious plant, and when the toxic effects were counteracted, it was a green winter weed that could be used to a great advantage in the overall operation of a sheep ranch in the weed-infested country.

The favorable result that we had gotten so far on this range experiment had caused people from far and near to be encouraging in their conversation when they were talking to me, and I heard numerous good reports from all phases of the ranching industry, including the bankers and loan companies, who were glad that there was a possibility of relief for yellowweed shrinkage and death loss in the near future. I hoped I at least had the good wishes of other research personnel in the Southwest until Mr. Damron, who was superintendent of the State and Federal Sonora Experiment Station, came to Fort Stockton to be one of the speakers at a 4-H all-day short course that was held in Rooney Park.

Tom Bond, a native of Sonora, had previously worked with Mr. Damron at the Sonora Experiment Station but had moved to Pecos County and was ranching west of town. He was helping the boys stage this day program. I went by in the afternoon to pay him my respects and visit for a few minutes during a break in the program and learned that several people had already told Mr. Damron about the yellowweed experiment. In my presence, Tom Bond volunteered that he had seen the sheep on the weed several times and had never seen any signs of sickness. He offered to take Mr. Damron out and show him the sheep; the pasture was only a few miles away and it would have been convenient after the program was over. However, Mr. Damron took a very negative attitude and said he wasn't interested in the experiment. This was somewhat of a shock to me, but at the time I only gave it passing notice and went on tending to my practice and my research.

I had ground several hundred pounds of fresh yellowweed in my laboratory through the years that I had been researching the weed and had developed the habit of waking up at about two o'clock in the morning—at that hour my mind was clear and there was no outside interference. This is when I would test the pulp and juices with various sorts of chemical combinations and use processes of crystallization on the liquids that I had extracted, none of which had as yet yielded any inkling as to the toxic substance of the weed. At the same time, it seemed, from the progress of the sheep on test, that by trial and error this forty-seventh formula was performing beautifully, but I still didn't have positive knowledge as to the toxic substance.

This particular morning I had filtered out 500 cc.'s of yellowweed juice using a porcelain filter and very fine filter paper. About daylight, Henry Scruggs from the West-Pyle Cattle Company pounded on my door and hollered at me to open up. When I opened the door, the office reeked with the sickening smell of yellowweed and he said, "Doc, you've been on that yellowweed so much I can smell it on your breath."

He had a stud that had been bitten over the nose by a rattlesnake and this kind of a call put me under pressure to get there before the swelling smothered the horse. In my rush to leave the office, I reached over and dropped a glass stopper in the 500-cc. vial of greenish liquid.

A trip to the West-Pyle Company was about one hundred and twenty miles round trip, and if you did any work or any visiting, the call would usually use up half a day. By the time I got back to town, the drugstores had taken several other calls for me, and I was kept busy for about three days and nights and didn't have time to pay any attention to my research.

I waked up about two o'clock on the fourth night after Scruggs had come by for me, and I thought I would throw out the old dried yellowweed that I had last ground and clean up my laboratory. After all the many attempts that I had made to work the liquid extract from yellowweed, I had never attempted to bottle and leave it for any period of time. To my surprise, the solids from the liquid of the yellowweed had gently settled to the bottom of the vial.

There was more than a half inch in depth of crystalline

substance that, at room temperature and without any effort on my part, had dropped out from the liquid substance. I very carefully poured off the liquid in another vial and then, by adding a small amount of triple-distilled water to the crystals, I very gently agitated the crystal away from the bottom of the vial and poured them into a porcelain onyx-lined crystallization dish. I placed this dish about two feet away from the heat element of a dehydration lamp. When it was thoroughly dry, it was an off-white color with a very faint greenish tinge.

After I had worked with yellowweed these years, I had lost some of my caution about toxic substances, and without giving a thought to the possible toxic content of the dried crystals, I dampened my finger and took a fair taste of it in my mouth. Some pharmacists can identify as many as four or five hundred botanical drugs by smell and taste, and a laboratory technician can ofttimes identify one hundred or more substances by the same method. In my life's experiences in the livestock business and practice of veterinary medicine, I had eaten about every kind of vegetable substance that cattle, sheep, or horses would eat, but this was a new one, and I had no taste experience that compared with these crystals.

There were almost enough crystals to fill a No. 10 horse capsule. These empty capsules were of gelatin substance and would not cause a chemical reaction, so I filled a capsule, put it in my vest pocket, got in my car, and drove to the airport at Midland, and sent it to a laboratory in New York City where I knew an old laboratory technician who I knew could identify the contents of the capsule. Two days later I received an airmail special-delivery letter identifying the properties contained in the crystals from yellowweed.

This, to my certain knowledge, was the first time that the substance had ever been isolated and identified. This was valuable information and could I have found it earlier would have greatly shortened the time, expense, and trouble I had spent evolving the formula that I was feeding to the experimental sheep. However, by the trial-and-error process, I already had developed the right formula and I made no changes after I knew what the toxic substance was.

For the next several weeks the only development was fat sheep. At the end of sixty days, the weed had begun to diminish and other vegetation had started to grow, so I cut these sheep off of feed and left them for forty-four days more and none became sick. They continued to gain weight, which brought up the argument of the possibility that a long period of medication might develop some immunity to continued grazing on yellowweed. For the last month there was little or no additional gain in the sheep and they were still fat, but the weed began to dry up, so we decided to ship them to market.

George Baker from the *Fort Stockton Pioneer* newspaper, who also had ranching interests, went out with us to round up the sheep when we decided to ship them. George gathered his own story from the fat sheep which were rounded up from the hills and draws that were a solid blanket of yellow since the weed had matured, toughened, and was in full bloom. The fat sheep were proof that yellowweed was a nutritious plant and that the medical formula had neutralized its ill effects and caused the weed to be looked at in a different light by those who owned yellowweed pastures. Although the war was over, technical materials were still hard to get and George did not have the film to take pictures of these sheep; but he gave a very accurate write-up in the *Fort Stockton Pioneer*.

Oscar Cain had half a carload and let us ship this bunch of fat yellowweed sheep in the top deck of his railroad car. He was shipping a different class of sheep from the experimental sheep, and even though they did not get mixed, if they had done so it would have been easy to separate them.

The sheep averaged 93½ pounds and averaged $11.01 a head and fifty-six of the better sheep brought 13¢ a pound, which was the top price for fat sheep the day and the week that they went to Fort Worth.

There had been some speculation around town and among people who knew about the experiment as to whether such a prolonged period of medication would affect the flavor and quality of the mutton from these sheep. There was also some doubts as to the flavor of the mutton that had grazed on yellowweed for this length of time.

When I brought these sheep to town to ship them, I cut out a big, aged, fat mutton. This one was probably the fattest sheep in the bunch. I asked my friend Marcus if he would like to have a fat sheep barbecue for his and my friends over at the goat ropin' next Saturday night at M. R. Gonzalez's Rancho Grande. He said that they would "shore be much obliged," so I told him to go up to the stock pens and butcher that mutton and all I wanted him to bring me was the liver.

Early the next morning before it got hot, Marcus came to the office with the liver wrapped up in brown paper and told me that was the fattest mutton he had ever butchered in all his life. I cut a little piece off the liver and did some laboratory testing on it for the possible accumulation of drugs. An excess of any prolonged medication that is harmful will sometimes be stored in the liver. However, the laboratory analysis showed no presence of any foreign substance. I wrapped the liver and put it in refrigeration until Marcus had the big barbecue at the goat ropin'.

I went to the goat ropin' next Saturday night and had a little barbecue and watched the crowd that had eaten the mutton for a little while and went back to the office and went to sleep.

The next day I took the liver up to Mrs. Carthuren's Café early in the morning and asked her to cook it and smother it in onions, and I would bring some friends up for dinner. About eleven o'clock I went to look around for loafers that I didn't feel would go home for dinner. I saw Boog Crisman and Snakey Price sittin' down in front of the pool hall. I walked up and told them that I was feeling pretty big-hearted that day and was tired of eatin' by myself, so I was invitin' them to Mrs. Carthuren's Café for dinner. Of course, it didn't take any argument to get this done. Before we got up to the café, I had picked up three more takers.

I was takin' a chance that they would order liver, and I had told Mrs. Carthuren not to let on if they didn't, just to feed them whatever they wanted. As we came in and lined up on one side of the counter, I said, "Mrs. Carthuren, that smells like some of your good liver and onions, and if it is, just bring me a bait of it." All the boys followed suit and said they would like some of that too.

Mrs. Carthuren was a little bitty woman who ran a real nice small café and her cooking was always good. She served up huge plates of liver and onions, hot rolls, French-fried potatoes, and iced tea. Some of the boys had seconds on the liver and bragged on the cookin'. Since it was summer and in the heat of the day, we all scattered to take our siesta. Now, I already knew that that meat didn't hurt the bunch over at the Rancho Grande ropin', and I was too tough for that liver to hurt me even if it was bad.

Along in the late afternoon, my dinner time friends began to come out into the shade and gather at the coffee grounds. By the time I had made it around and visited with all of them, they were still braggin' about what a good dinner we had and that was the best liver they ever "et." I gently broke the news to them that the liver was from a yellowweed sheep. None of them showed any signs of turning pale and all of them laughed and commented that they believed all sheep ought to have yellowweed and Doc Green's feed before they was butchered. We had a big laugh and decided that we had settled the question, and there was no doubt that yellowweed affected the meat of a sheep unless it made it better.

The spring crop of yellowweed had gotten tough, but the hot summer sun had stopped the growth of other vegetation. Old sheep will eat tough weed before lambs will and I was trying to get all the evidence during this grazing year. We turned a second flock of sheep in the same pasture, one hundred and twenty Rommeldale ewes.

They were grazed and fed on the same medication for thirty days and then were taken off the feed for seven days. During this period of seven days, one died and twenty-seven became sick in varying degrees. The sick sheep were put on medicated feed, and after three days all but one recovered. They were left on feed sixty days before the weed completely played out for the season.

YELLOWWEED CURE

I had bought up all the available drugs to compound this 1,400 pounds of feed that had been fed successfully to the last flock of sheep. There was a good healthy interest among the ranchers, and a number of them wanted to feed some of the medicated feed to their sheep the coming winter if we had sufficient early rainfall to make yellowweed.

I felt that the last experimental sheep had compiled enough proof and evidence that there would be a demand for some medicated feed to be fed on a commercial basis, and it was way past time for me to begin to get some of the money back for the several years of research. I was aware that the drugs were an expensive additive to the cost of feed, and I knew that I had to go to the original source of supply to buy quantities for later-date shipments in order for the drug-refining companies to be able to give me the best possible price.

In late summer we began to get some good rains that assured an early yellowweed crop that fall. Through correspondence with the larger drug houses, I had been told that in order to get the drugs that had to be shipped by water from other points of the world, I would have to go to New York City to establish priority through the proper channels for cargo space for a low freight bearing raw-drug material.

After my summer practice had begun to slack off and before the fall rush began, I got my business in order and drove to New York City for the sole purpose of arranging for raw-drug-bearing materials to be shipped by water freight to the processors in New York who would extract and refine the drug substances. The major drug supplier was perfectly willing to cooperate in securing and refining these drugs from their original source in the tropical islands. However, I was asking for more of these drugs than there had ever been any common demand for, and the drug

company said that they would have to have a marginal cash advance before they would be interested in stocking items that heretofore had only been on demand in nominal quantities. I called Dow Puckett, and he wired me the cash needed to make the contract final. This took a matter of two or three days, and I turned around and started back to the Far Southwest.

In the fall yellowweed was making its appearance in sufficient quantities for everybody to know that it would be a yellowweed year and it would be impossible to run sheep in many of the pastures unless they were fed yellowweed feed.

Feed mills had begun to take a different attitude toward my research and the story of the success with last year's sheep had been widespread, and I began to make arrangements for the milling of this feed. Olin Childs, the Purina feed dealer in Fort Stockton, and Mr. Buckingham, the district representative who lived in San Angelo, contacted me about having this medication compounded into their grain-cube feed instead of putting it into soybean or cottonseed protein meals. There would be as much as $20 a ton difference in the cost of the feed stuff that went into the finished product, and several of the ranchers who were more interested in the medication than they were in the feed supplement were very much in favor of putting it in grain cubes and saving the difference per ton.

Between the ranchers and the Purina Company we agreed to buy a hundred tons of grain-cube feed medicated with my formula. The New York drug firms delivered as per their contract in ample time for me to compound the drugs and haul them by truck to Fort Worth where Purina's mill operation was based.

I wanted the drug mixed with the grain feeds in a batch mixer 2,000 pounds at a time, but Purina had installed some highly scientific and expensive automatic mixing equipment that was described as having a "magic electric eye." The drugs could be mixed with the feed as it moved through various chutes on the way to the cubing machine, which would put the final finish on the feed. I didn't like this idea and didn't necessarily approve the proposal, but their argument was that this continuous flow with the "magic electric eye" would be the only way that the mill could handle it. They assured me that there was not the slightest possibility of error in the milling with this "magic electric eye" controlling the flow of the various ingredients.

I stayed in Fort Worth until we finished the milling of the hundred tons, which amounted to three boxcar loads. After it was sealed and turned over to the railroad, I drove back to Fort Stockton to be there to unload the feed when it arrived. The ranchers who were interested were all glad to receive the feed early and have it in their barns ready to use when the yellowweed symptoms would first begin to appear in their sheep.

'Most all the flocks had been put on feed a week to ten days before Christmas and apparently were doing all right, and I felt like it was safe for me to take off and go home to have Christmas with my folks. It was five hundred and thirty-five miles to Cumby, and took me a day to drive home. I stayed Christmas Day and drove back the third day, and the next morning several flocks of sheep were showing sickness.

Some flocks were not eating the medicated feed and were getting sick due to the absence of the medication in their daily diet of yellowweed. Other flocks were eating all the feed everyday that was given them and were getting progressively sicker. Then there were a few more sheep that got sick later but not seriously so.

The best thing that I could do at the time was to buy

fresh unmedicated feed and deliver it to the ranchers and take up all the medicated feed and haul it back to town. All the ranchers had to move their sheep off the yellow-weed pastures. Everybody was kind and considerate and thoughtful of me, and I did not receive any abuse or bad publicity from the ranchers that were feeding the feed because they had seen the sheep the year before and were all willing to believe that something had gone wrong. However, the diehards and smart alecks were having quite a celebration at my expense up and down the streets and at the conversation places. Their capital remark was that they "knowed it wouldn't work when they went to sure 'nuff usin' it on ranches."

After the feed was in storage in town, I began to take samples. The color varied from no medication to feed that was solid black with medicine and so hard that the sheep wouldn't eat it and had gotten sick. The feed that had little or no medicine color to it didn't contain enough medication and those sheep got sick. This left a few flocks where the drug content appeared to be all right, but they had slowly sickened too.

I ground, washed, and burned feed and determined that this great "magic electric eye" must have gotten sick on medicine and the entire hundred tons was badly out of proportion, and unless something could be done, my year's supply of drugs and another yellowweed season was about to be lost. We had been reporting this condition to Mr. Buckingham by phone in San Angelo for two or three weeks, and he was dodging the issue and hadn't brought himself to face the music and tell the mill and his superiors about the great "magic electric eye."

During this time I had discovered another serious fault with fibrous cubed feed. When the drugs were compounded into soybean or cottonseed protein meal and made into pellets, the protein meal released the medical properties in the stomach of the sheep, which counteracted the toxic substance from yellowweed as it first entered the animal's digestive tract. Now, when the grain cube entered the sheep's stomach, the grain and fiber swelled and reabsorbed the gastric juices and reabsorbed the medical properties and was passed on into the small intestine for digestion and thereby removed the medical properties from the stomach, which was the site of action where the toxic substance had to be neutralized. This explained why the sheep that were on fairly well-proportioned feed gradually sickened.

I got on the phone one night and jarred the Purina Company from St. Louis to Fort Worth to Mr. Buckingham. The next morning when I opened my office, Mr. Buckingham was in Fort Stockton. We loaded all the feed that was left from this "magic electric eye" mistake in two railroad cars and shipped it back to the mill at Fort Worth. All the cubes were reground into meal form and by some rare unbelievable circumstance, it was discovered that there were still some batch mixers in Purina's plant that must have been overlooked in the beginning.

After the meal was all milled and completely remixed it was necessary to determine what the percentage of medical properties now amounted to. I gathered up samples of the meal and went to a laboratory in Fort Worth where I knew the technician; I felt sure he would help me find the proper content.

He suggested that we burn this meal in airtight drums in the absence of oxygen and thereby analyze the char, and at the same time we would do a wash-out flotation on some of the other meal. By these two and other processes we determined that the protein content was greatly diminished from the original 20 per cent and that the drug content was in overabundance due to the fact that the sheep had eaten up the cubes that had contained very little medication, so I told the mill to add 27½ per cent of the total volume in soybean meal.

We remilled this mixture and shipped it back to Fort Stockton, but by this time the yellowweed was almost over and much of this feed lay in the barns on the ranches through the summer and turned rancid and was worthless by the following yellowweed season.

This was the most serious blow in time and finances that I had suffered in my years of research and even though I had a staunch following of believers, I had lost a year and had failed to gain any more support, and needless to say and without blame to them, had lost quite a few of those who had been interested the year before.

I was at the El Sinora Cattle Company one day later that summer doing surgery on some Hereford bulls' eyes. We worked these bulls into heavy constructed cattle chutes that were intended to be used for branding, dehorning, and any other surgical operation that might be necessary. The gate on the end of the chute was made in such a manner that a cow's or bull's head could be stuck out at the top of the gate without the bull being able to get away. We would place a rope on the bull's horns and sometimes shape a halter around his nose and a cow hand would pull his head whichever direction was necessary for me to perform surgery on an eye.

During the day I noticed twenty three-year-old fillies in the corral next to the chutes where we were working the bulls. These were real nice fillies that had been selected to keep as replacement mares that the ranch raised their cow horses from. I especially liked one filly and H. H. Matthews sold her to me for cash, and I told him I'd pick her up at a later date.

One afternoon when I wasn't busy, I called Peeler Matthews, who was the foreman, and told him that if he could get the horses in the corral, I would bring my horse trailer and come get the one I had bought. This was all right with him, so I talked my friend Gid into going along and helping me with her. It was a short trip of only about twenty miles, and I explained that Peeler would have the horses in the corral and we would be back in the middle of the afternoon.

The horses were in the corral when we got there and Peeler roped the filly that I had bought from horseback. Gid quickly stepped up to Peeler on foot and took the rope off the saddlehorn and shook the filly some slack. Peeler sat on his horse and I sat on the fence and we both wondered what Gid was about to do.

He tossed the loose end of the lariat rope on the ground and walked up to the filly, apparently had quite a little conversation with her, reached up and pulled the lariat rope off over her head and dropped it on the ground. After he scratched her under the neck, he sat down in front of her, leaned back on her forelegs, and got pretty well acquainted with the "little dear," as he called her. He put a hackamore on her and fastened it very loosely. Gid left the hackamore rope lying on the ground, walked around the filly, never taking his hands off her, spanked her on the flank, pulled her tail in a friendly sort of way, and finally got up on her back. He stretched out with his chin resting on her withers and crossed his boots over her rump.

He later dismounted by sliding off over her hindquarters and told his newfound friend that he would like for her to go home with him. He put his arm over her shoulders, picked up the hackamore rope, and he and she walked out of the corral to the trailer.

While this was going on, a bunch of Mexican ranch hands had gathered around the corral fence. They neither spoke nor understood much English, but one of them asked Peeler Matthews "How he did it?" Peeler told them in Spanish that Gid could hypnotize a horse and that he could do it to a man the same way. As we started out toward the trailer, I noticed that all the Mexican cowboys had disappeared.

In the fall yellowweed was not making a vigorous growth because there were large areas that had not received any rain. However, there had been rain in the draws where there had been overflow and the yellowweed there was lush. A few of my prospective customers were not willing to take the bad results of the year before because of the mistake in the mixing of the feed and medicine as final, and we began to make plans to go back to batch-making the feed at the Minimax Mill at Lamesa and try to forget the nightmare of the magic eye.

I now had a source of supply established for the drugs that I needed. However, it was necessary to contact the wholesale drug refineries in the summer while raw drugs were available in order to have adequate supplies by fall. I had bought enough drugs to medicate another hundred tons of feed for several reasons. First, I felt that we would use another hundred tons of feed that year and, second, it was necessary to buy in this quantity to get the best possible prices on drugs.

It was a dry fall and even in the lush places ranchers were slow to start feeding and were hoping against hope that maybe yellowweed wouldn't be as early as usual. When sheep started getting sick in December, I began mixing drugs at Fort Stockton, where I had them stored, and I hauled the compounded drugs by trailer and pickup load one hundred and forty-five miles to Lamesa. A pickup load of drugs would medicate about a truckload of feed, and the mill would deliver it back to me in Fort Stockton.

This was a long, slow process, but every flock of sheep on feed were doing good and I was on the road back to regaining the confidence in the project that I had before the feed mistake of the previous year. Very few sheep on the medicated feed got sick, but the lack of winter and spring rains caused the weed to play out, and some of the flocks did not have to be fed over as long a period of time since the yellowweed season was cut short.

This left me with about 70 per cent of the newly purchased drugs on hand. I had lost $9,000 in drugs and feed the year of the magic-eye mistake, and now I had several thousand dollars' worth of drugs on hand at the end of the season and the old-time desert ranchers had begun looking at the sky and talking about drouth.

I was walking through the lobby of the hotel headed for the dining room one day, and there were two or three loafers in the lobby who were opposed to anybody doing good, and one of them said to the other, "Between the failures of yellowweed and the drouth, this season will just about bury old Doc."

Beco Price, an old-time cowboy, was sittin' across from them with his back to the wall and I heard him say, "They'd better bury him face down or he's liable to claw out."

There were still some occasional rains east of the Pecos River in the Ozona and Sonora country, but west of the Pecos was now in a drouth. Ranch people by nature are optimists and spirits were still high, and when dry weather was mentioned, somebody would chime out, "It always has rained, and it will rain again by the time that we 'have to have it.'" However, the old men who had ranched the country for a lifetime knew that a drouth in the Trans-Pecos Region of Texas didn't necessarily have to be broken when the young people and newcomers thought it "had to be."

The following winter there was no sign of any weeds, good or bad, and the old vegetation had mostly been eaten up by the cattle and sheep. It was the general hope of all ranchers to hang on until it rained, and the first attempt at staying was made by buying alfalfa hay to feed during that winter. As baby lambs were born in the spring and as the days got hotter and the nights got shorter and the lambs got smaller, the first movement of livestock started.

Many ranchers went east of the Pecos River where it was still raining and leased pastures and shipped off of their desert ranches. 'Most everyone began to sell off the old and the cull end of their cattle, sheep, and horses. I had mares and colts and young unbroken horses pastured out with ranchers all over the country, and occasionally there would be a little thunder cloud come up and rain somewhere on a half section of land. It got to be a common joke around town that "it rained on Doc Green's horses," because I had some stock in any direction.

Ranchers are a hardy breed, but there were other winters without winter weeds and other springs without grass coming, and between feed bills, short wool clips, and the lack of lamb and calf crops, the Trans-Pecos Region had less livestock, more broke ranchers, no use for medicated yellowweed, and less need for the services of the village horse doctor.

Yellowweed had been a threat to the ranching of sheep west of the Pecos River ever since man stocked the country. It will always be the principal killer of sheep in the Trans-Pecos Region, and I doubt seriously that there will ever be a magic wand that you can wave from the top of a windmill or a miracle spray that will eliminate yellowweed.

In my earliest research, I planted the seeds of yellowweed in a flower box and moved the box several times through the years and pulled the weed from it, never letting one plant seed for twenty-three years. The yellowweed seed bed lays in the alkaline soils of the desert region, immune to any chemical reaction, and under sparse rainfall, 5 per cent of it will last for more than thirty years. Since one yellowweed plant can make as many as forty thousand seed, I can never believe that drouth will endure long enough or any man-made preparation will ever destroy the yellowweed seed bed of the Trans-Pecos Region of Texas and will always be a problem.

PINGUEY, FEVER
AND THE QUEEN

I hadn't had any long-distance calls from New Mexico after the poison-corn call until the Navaho Indian agent wrote me a letter asking about information I had gained on the poison plants that the sheep had been eating on the Hubble Ranch back in the spring.

He was referring to some weed problems that the Hubble Ranch Company had called me in on for consultation when they had some sheep under herd north of Quemado and Pie Town that were in a short dieout, and with the other young fresh spring weeds coming, the dieout took care of itself. I had such a short time to work on their troubles that I really didn't make any worthwhile finds while I was there.

Since I had no real information that I could put in a letter, I telephoned the agent and explained to him that my suspicions were that pinguey was the weed that had caused the trouble at Hubble. However, due to the short time I had to work on it, I had no real information and would welcome the opportunity to continue my research if they were having sufficient trouble on the Navaho Reservation for them to justify having me come up there.

Due to the prolonged drouth, my practice was so light that I was glad for some work among the Navaho at the government's expense, and at the same time, the information I was compiling might be of use in my future practice.

Research is always time-consuming and expensive, especially so where desert plants are involved. Outside of a nervous mental curiosity, the only other justifiable reason for such time

and expense is that there's always the possibility and probability that you are better qualifying yourself for future cases in your practice.

We agreed that I should get up there as soon as convenient and start work since they were already having more than the usual amount of death loss for that time of the winter. It took me a few days to turn all my horses out into big pastures where they didn't need to be looked after and spread the word that I would be in New Mexico probably until Christmas.

When I got to the Navaho Reservation, the agent said it would be well for me to set up whatever laboratory equipment that I needed at their headquarters in Gallup. I had no idea whether that was good or bad, so I went along with his suggestion that he provide me with sufficient space, and I began to work among the affected flocks. Almost all of them were from sixty to a hundred miles from Gallup.

All these sheep were under herd and the Indian sheepherders were very observant. After they decided that I wasn't a smart aleck, which took them awhile, they began to volunteer good information as to the eating habits of their sheep; they also knew the different families of weeds growing on the range where their particular flocks would be.

For a few weeks I was learning more about Indian lore than I was about sheep. However, I was no stranger to the Navaho and had bought horses from them many years before I had begun the practice of veterinary medicine.

I was in a flock of sheep in the Zuni Mountains. An old herder told me that the youngest ewes here would get sick first and later the old mutton sheep that they kept around to shear and eat might get a little sick but would live a long time. When they moved the herd to new range, many of the big old mutton would get well.

This information in itself meant that it was fresh, tender

weeds that were causing the trouble because the youngest sheep ate the tenderest feed and it would not be from brushy growth where the bark or seeds might be poison. I gathered some specimens of the different types of vegetation that were growing in the mountains at this time of year and went back to my temporary laboratory to do a little analyzing.

I explained to the Indian agent one morning that I would have to "post" several sheep in order to determine what type of poisoning was involved. He said that he would put out the word among the herders and make it all right with them for me to do this. I had begun to learn that a flock of these sheep might belong to as many as eight or ten or even more Indians, and that they took time about herding, and that they had different earmarks and other means of identifying their sheep.

A few days later, I drove to Sheep Springs, I guess about forty miles north of Gallup, to see a herd that had been reported as having some sick sheep. I got there about the time they brought the flock in from the hills to the Indian settlement and I saw a sheep in the bunch that showed symptoms of being sick. I told the herder that I wanted to kill that sheep and asked him to catch him while I went to the car to get some instruments.

The car was maybe a hundred yards away and when I got back, he had a sheep hung up by one hind leg in a mesquite tree with his throat cut. I didn't think it was the one I had pointed out, so I looked around through the herd and saw that the sick sheep was not the one he had caught. I didn't make any mention of this, thinkin' I might find some symptoms in the sheep that he had hung up.

When the sheep was dead and had quit bleeding, I told the Indian to lay him on the ground, where I could tell more about his insides when I cut him open. While this short conversation went on, a whole bunch of Indian squaws and little kids gathered at my back without me knowing that they had gotten there.

I laid this sheep open and looked at his liver and spleen and kidneys and took a sample of fresh-eaten stuff from his first stomach, then got up off my knees. The herder asked me if I was through with him and I nodded my head and walked to the car.

Out of curiosity I decided to go back and see what was goin' to happen to the sheep, but I was really a little too late to tell. That flock of squaws had stripped the hide off him, had cut him up, and had disappeared to their hogans; and there were a few small children still in sight, eating chunks of raw liver out of their bare hands.

I went back to the laboratory and worked on this mass of green stuff that I had taken from the sheep's paunch, putting it through a short lab process I used—rather a force of habit than really hunting for something, as I knew the digestive process could have made chemical reactions and I didn't expect to find anything worthwhile.

The next morning I went to another flock of sheep that were being herded near Crown Point and had been moved from Standing Rock because they had been getting sick on that range. This time I found a sheep that was really sick and told the herder to catch him and hold him until I got back from the car where I needed to get some instruments.

Sure 'nuff this herder had caught and killed the wrong sheep. After I had seen that other one evaporate with a bunch of squaws, I decided it wouldn't hurt for him to have two dead sheep, so I made him catch the sick one. By now there were about fifteen squaws there who I guess came out of the rocks, and there was a good deal of gruntin' and head shakin' going on, and this herder didn't want to kill this sick sheep.

There are always some Indians who have been sent to reservation schools and can speak good English. They would grunt and make signs and talk Indian to each other, and if I could get one to say anything to me, it would be in English, but this particular bunch all of a sudden lost their education. When I told the herder to kill the sick sheep, nobody could understand what I meant, so I stepped astraddle the sheep and held his shoulders with my knees and turned his head up with one hand and cut his throat with the other. When I glanced up at the Indian squaws, I recognized their blank expressions as being ones of disgust and contempt.

I told the herder not to touch the sheep that was hanging in the tree and I began to post the one on the ground. I found some enlarged welp-like spots on the liver and a darkened spleen. Then I turned to the sheep in the tree and told the herder to lay him on the ground.

It was noticeable that the squaws didn't touch the poor, sick sheep that I had just finished with, but when I got through looking at the fat sheep, they nearly had a fight among themselves as they skinned, quartered, and carried off the fat sheep. Those who had been pushed back and hadn't gotten a chance at that good mutton turned and cut up the poor one and went off with it.

The next morning I was telling the Indian agent at Gallup about this little scuffle and about the two different herders killing the wrong sheep. He explained to me that under their ration rules they were not supposed to be butchering any of their breeding flock and that the Indian sheepherder was still smarter than a white man because he wanted to kill a fat sheep so they could eat him and have good mutton whether or not I found out what I wanted to know from the post-mortem.

He thought this was funny and told me that I might

know a lot about medicine, but I needed to smarten up about Indians. I thought this was a little funny myself, but I started making plans to hold my own the next time me and my red brothers did any sheep work together.

The next bunch of sick sheep that I went into were back up near Toadlena on a primitive road. I wanted to post a sick sheep and since there were several in the flock, I told the herder for him and his dogs to hold them up in a tight band. I walked into them and took the sick sheep that I wanted by the hind leg and pulled him out of the bunch.

I stood over him and cut his throat, and when he quit kicking I laid him out on a big, clean, flat rock that was almost an ideal operating table. His internal organs confirmed the last sick sheep I posted and furnished some further evidence of vegetable poison.

When I told the herder goodbye and left the flock, no squaws had shown up for the sick sheep that I had killed and I don't know whether or not any came out of the rocks after I left.

There had been some little snow flurries of no major importance and most of the snow had melted a few days after it had fallen, which caused a slightly better assortment of small weeds to start coming to the top of the ground. I had begun to get some fairly good ideas about their troubles, and for the next several days I gathered and ground the pinguey weed and was working at isolating the toxic substances.

It was almost Christmastime and I told the Indian agent that I would lock up my office and go home for the Christmas holidays and would be back soon after the first of January.

The sunshiny, balmy winter days of the desert cause people who are simple enough to be fishermen to go fishing

in the Rio Grande River in the Big Bend country, and Frank
Hinde was one of these people.

Frank's wife, Ruth, had gone to Oklahoma City to see
her mother and Frank had promised faithfully that he
would not go to the river. However, Lige Warnock and
some more of his other cronies came up with the proposition and, knowing that Ruth would be gone for several
days, Frank didn't see any harm in goin' fishin'.

They camped on the Rio Grande River several miles up-
stream from the trading post at Lajitas. Fishing was good,
the weather was nice, and they were having a big time.

Frank was six feet eight inches tall and well proportioned, and of course, all his fishing partners were much
smaller men. The day they decided to come home, Frank
went into the river to do some grabbling along the banks
for the big ones that might be in the rock holes in the water
too deep for the other fishermen to get to.

By the time he drove the one hundred and seventy-five
miles home, it was late afternoon and he was running a
little fever. The next day he was sick enough that he went
to bed without anybody tellin' him to. He lay there long
enough to get worried about himself, and he called Lige
Warnock to ask him to find the village horse doctor to
have me come and look at him.

I had been to my folks at Cumby, Texas, for Christmas
and it was late afternoon when I drove into town and Lige
saw me. We went up to Frank's house, which was in the
farwestern part of town. He had a great big rambling
house, and nearly everybody in West Texas drives up to
the back door and goes in.

Frank was in the back bedroom, and due to his size, his
bed had been specially made and was extra long. He was
lying there in his longhandle underwear in cold weather,

kickin' the cover off, and had a raging fever. I talked to him a few minutes; then I went back to my car and got my stethoscope and listened to his heart and lungs.

He said, "Well, fool, I didn't call you up here for company. What's the matter with me?"

I said, "Well, me and the rest of the boys will go have our blue serge suits cleaned and pressed and some will have to set the buttons over on their vests since they wore them last. This is Friday and you have virus pneumonia, and you've got it bad, and you ain't goin' to take no medicine or cover up or do anything that anybody tells you, and you've already told all of us not to call Ruth, so I'd say by Tuesday, you'll be deader than hell and we'll have to wear them dark suits."

We hadn't been able to keep the cover on him and he reached down to the foot of the bed, pulled up the blanket under his chin and said, "My, God, call the old lady."

Then, he said, "Why don't ya give me something? You gonna let me lay here and die for the lack of medical attention?"

Aureomycin was a new drug and was not readily available. The advanced literature on it indicated that it was at that time the most effective antibiotic to treat virus pneumonia. By my various connections in research, I always managed by some devious means to have the latest so-called wonder drugs, and I had a good supply to use on Frank Hinde.

The prescribed treatment was two capsules the first dose and one capsule every three hours thereafter for about twenty-four hours. Well, I knew old Frank was nearer the size of a horse than he was a man, so I gave him four the first dose and two every three hours thereafter.

I told the rest of the boys who had gathered around (they were all old men) that they could go home and go to bed and I would go in the other bedroom and spend the night with my patient. I took the alarm clock in the bedroom and when it would go off every three hours, I would raise up and holler for Frank to take his medicine.

About the third time I hollered that night, he didn't answer. I said to myself, I never have gone to sleep and let a horse die. I wonder if I've gone to sleep and let a man and a half die.

I slipped my boots on and walked into the bedroom and Frank had gone to sleep and the bed covers were wringin' wet with sweat which, of course, meant that the fever had broke. I changed the covers on him and kept givin' him medicine for the rest of the night.

Ruth had a big linen closet full of nice clean linens and every time I got a fresh batch, I threw the ones I took off in a corner of the room. By morning I had all the corners of that great big bedroom covered up with wadded-up sheets thrown against the wall. My patient was well, with no fever, no sweat, and damn little color. He had quit cussin' me and was really too weak to brag on me, but was awful proud to be alive.

In the meantime Ruth had landed at the airport at Midland, which was a hundred and ten miles away, and Lige had gone over there after her. I had never used female nurses in my large-animal practice and didn't care to be around when she saw her husband (and my patient) after this siege of sickness and miracle medicine administered by the eminent horse doctor.

Albert Kay came in about sunup and I told him I believed I'd go and tend to my more pleasant large-animal practice, and if Frank wanted some breakfast, he could fix it for him. Soon after that, Lige and Ruth came in and when Ruth walked in the room and saw all them dirty sheets and saw Frank layin' there kind of an ash color, sensitive womanlike that she was she nearly came apart and asked him if he had had the doctor.

She, knowing that he never went to a doctor, asked, "Who did you have?"

He said, "Doc Green."

Well, she blowed all to pieces and broke to the telephone and called a young doctor that was just out of the army, Ben McReynolds. In fact, he was still wearing his army uniform on calls. He was a nice little fellow with a kind, quiet bedside manner and a cute little mustache.

Ruth met him at the front door and as he came down the hall, she was explaining to him the awful thing that had happened and that she sure hoped that Frank wasn't so far gone that he couldn't save him. The little young doctor had never seen Frank standing up and didn't know how big he was and when he walked into the room and looked from the foot of the bed to the head of it, he thought he was lookin' up the highway.

Ruth told Frank who the young doctor was. In cowboy fashion, Frank said, "I'm glad to meet ya. Have a seat."

Dr. McReynolds pulled up a chair and in his very best manner asked Frank a few simple questions and then began to examine him. He asked Frank whether I gave him any medicine and Frank said, "Yep, and it sure got the job done. I was sick as hell this time yesterday."

The young doctor asked, "How do you feel now?"

"I ain't got a pain. I'm just weak and hungry as hell."

Dr. McReynolds asked, "Do you know what kind of medicine Dr. Green gave you?"

Well, I had known this was comin' so I had left the empty vials from the medicine we had used up under the corner of Frank's mattress close to his head and told him not to throw 'em away. So, he told the young doctor, "Yeah, he left these empty bottles," as he reached under the mattress and handed him a big handful of empty bottles.

Dr. McReynolds studied the labels and the quantities, got up out of the chair, pushed it back to the corner and said, "Mr. Hinde, you are a well man."

All during that time Ruth had been taking on about how foolish it was to call me for a human being. The young doctor turned to Ruth and said, "Mrs. Hinde, you will never realize how fortunate you were to get Dr. Green on this case."

Ruth burst into another fit and said, "What do you mean by that?"

He said, "I mean to tell you that I would never have known the dosage required for an animal of this size."

I left in early January and went back to the Indian reservation in New Mexico to continue my work on the sick Navajo sheep. I had determined that some of the toxic substance in pinguey was the same as that in yellowweed, and I took enough medicine to compound into the feed to run some experiments.

I explained to the Indian agent what I had in mind and he said that there would be more weed and it would be easier to get it pulled and fed to the sheep by a certain herder over at Nakaibito. He went over there with me and after visiting with the Indian and explaining what we wanted done, we went back to town.

I got some cottonseed meal and mixed the medicines that were in dry powder form into the meal. The next day the old Indian herder had a small corral ready for the sheep; it was built against a rock bluff with brush and cactus cut and piled on the other three sides for a fence. This corral was near a little spring from which he could carry water for them.

We took out of a flock ten grown ewes that you could plainly tell by the stain on their mouths were eating pinguay. These sheep had never been fed any kind of commercial feed, and it was necessary to pull fresh grown pinguay and dust cottonseed meal on it to get them to develop a taste for the feed. This was not real good because they were accumulating more poison while they were learning to eat feed.

This old Indian herder was a good sheepman, and with the patience of his breed, he managed to get them all to eating the medicated feed out of a trough within a week. This experimental bunch of sheep started with the handicap of already being on the weed. However, this was almost typical in that they would be on the weed before they would be sick enough to justify treatment—provided the drugs were going to be effective.

I don't know how many Indian kids the old Indian herder had pulling weed, but every time I was by to look at the sheep during the next three weeks, the pen would be bedded with dry wilted weed that had been left and there was always fresh weed that had just been pulled and given to them.

I stopped posting any sheep, and where flocks would get sick, I would advise that they be moved to some other range. Since they were under herd, this was not hard to do.

While I was killing time waiting on the little bunch of ewes that we were running the test on, I, true to my nature and in keeping with my weakness, went up around Shiprock and Farmington and bought a few Indian horses and sent them home by truck. This helped fill some time and, besides, I hadn't had any Indian horses in a few years and an old horseman always likes to change colors and models.

The sheep on feed got better and, in fact, had begun to get fat. I had the medical answer to the pinguey problem and decided to make a complete report to the Indian agent. He had been fully aware of all the details of the medicated meal and experiments that he had helped me set up with the old herder.

When we were talking about this work, he asked me to give him a written report for the government records of his Indian agency. I dictated and had this report typed out in good order and delivered it to his office and was making arrangements to pack up and leave. However, I had offered to help secure the necessary drugs and furnish them with the proper proportions and let them mix and feed it themselves.

In a day or two, the Indian agent read my report, asked for a bill for my services, told me he appreciated the information, and wound up his conversation by sayin' that it would be impractical because the Indians, the sheep, and the Indian Agency weren't interested in going into the business of "feeding" sheep.

Even though I was being paid for my services, I didn't appreciate this government attitude, so I packed my riggin' and told him that the sheep and the Indians didn't have as bad a case of poison as the damn Indian agent and said, "Goodbye!"

On a nice spring Sunday morning I was called out west of town where several good gentle horses had run through a barbed-wire fence during the night, which at the time appeared to be unexplainable. They were rather badly cut up on their forelegs and breasts. It was later proven by the owners of these horses that they were buzzed by some fly-boys in planes from the nearby training field at Fort Stockton, and this scared the horses into the fences. Horse hair was even found on the bellies of some of the airplanes in the investigation.

I sewed these horses up carefully, matching the muscle

as best as I could in each case and very carefully suturing the skin in such a pattern that drainage would not be a problem. I had used all the wound dressing that I had with me.

When I came back to town, I went by the office and washed up and just before noon went by the Stockton Pharmacy to give Joe Henson some prescriptions to be filled for the people who owned the horses; they would come in later and get the medicine for further treatment.

There was a beautiful lady in the drugstore who had just gotten into town; she had come in to tell Joe she was present and would be ready to start a cosmetic demonstration at the drugstore Monday morning. Well, cosmetic companies don't send out thick-hided, coarse-haired girls to demonstrate their products, so, needless to say, she looked to me like she would be real good company to take to lunch. It didn't take me more than a minute to make the proposition.

She was delighted and we went up to Beanie Christian's Dixie Café. The local Sunday diners were there and also a fair number of tourists, because Beanie ran a better-than-average West Texas café.

Beanie was a little fellow, past middle age, an old bachelor, very mild mannered, with a broken tremorlike voice. The natives were speculating about who Doc's new girl friend was and Beanie was more curious than he appeared to be. I saw him and one of his local customers gettin' their heads together, talkin' and smilin' and lookin' over our way.

When this cosmetic queen and I came up to pay the bill, she was standing that nice, proper social distance from my elbow. As Beanie looked at her, he said in a shaky voice, "Doc, your wife just called and said for you to come home and bring home paregoric for the baby."

Half the house began to laugh. It was funny to me that

old Beanie would take after me, as tough as I was known to be, verbally speakin', and for that split second, I was about to let him get away with his joke when I suddenly caught up the slack by saying, "No more certain than I am about the little devil, maybe you ought to take him that paregoric."

A second later he bumped his head on the kitchen door and wasn't seen for the rest of the day.

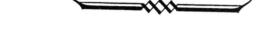

TROUBLE IN THE MOUNTAINS

It was early summer and I had moved out about fifteen miles from town and was living in a batchin' outfit on Dow Puckett's ranch. I had answered a call earlier in the day south of Sanderson and went to my batchin' outfit instead of going back to town that night.

Mr. Hill, who was foreman of the Hess Ranch a few miles north of Marathon, had been trying to reach me at Fort Stockton. When he couldn't get me he called Roger Gallemore at the drugstore. Roger told him that if I came in by closing time he would have me call him.

Roger forgot about the call and closed up and went to bed. He remembered during the night and tried to call me. Unbeknownst to me, the phone at my batchin' outfit was dead, and when Roger couldn't get me to answer, he called Punch McAdams, who lived at the old headquarters about three or four miles across the ranch from me. Roger told Punch about Mr. Hill's call and about my phone being dead, so Punch got in his pickup and drove over. He woke me up and told me my phone was dead and relayed the message from Mr. Hill.

I got up and drove to the Hess Ranch, and at about two o'clock in the morning I knocked on Mr. Hill's door and told him I had just gotten his call. He was a little surprised to see me and explained that he had not expected me to make an emergency call; he said that the horse had been affected

for several days. He invited me in, made a pot of coffee, and got dressed.

After a visit and his explainin' to me about the horse having abscesses on various parts of his body, we took lights and went out to the barn to look at the young stallion. He was a nice young horse that had been turned out in a small pasture on the south side of Iron Mountain. When Hill had noticed a large swelling on the point of his shoulder, he thought it was from a mare kicking him or some other accident and had brought him into the ranch headquarters. Hill said that he had lanced that abscess and within a week's time, several more had formed at other places.

As I examined the horse, I realized that I had found a new booger of some kind. This young stud was running very little or no temperature, and when I examined the flesh around these abscesses, he was not sensitive and very little soreness had developed. There was no indication of bruises or any signs of shotgun pellets, and the abscesses that I opened had no mesquite thorns or other foreign objects in them.

I told Mr. Hill that I didn't readily know what was the matter with the horse, but I'd sure try to find out. I took a blood specimen from his jugular vein for laboratory analysis. Penicillin had just been released for general use and was very expensive, costing fifteen dollars for a three-hundred-thousand-unit vial. I gave the horse as many vials as I thought necessary, and since this was a very valuable horse, Hill said to give him more if he needed it.

When I got to my office it was about daylight, a nice quiet time of day to do some undisturbed laboratory work. I centrifuged the blood, made a smear on a slide with some of it and put it under my microscope but did not find anything unusual. I did some laboratory tests on the clear serum and got no noticeable reaction.

By now the phone was ringing and the day had started. After a dull winter, my spring and summer practice was pushing me and all I had to do to start a busy day was to get my clothes and boots on and be within hearin' of the telephone or hollerin' distance of the people on the street. The cases of the day soon caused me to have to dismiss the Hess Ranch horse until I could get back to him.

I went to the Post Office and was opening my mailbox when Bobo stuck his head out of the service window, laughing, and said, "Doc, here's a postcard that's yours too."

Everybody in the Post Office was laughing about the card.

A few days before this, I had stopped at the drugstore in Sanderson and the druggist told me that a young woman who lived in town had a dog she wanted me to take a look at. It was just a few blocks off my run, so I went by. This young woman had a little baby of crawling age playing with the dog on the floor. The dog was a miniature breed and had some little pups; she wasn't exactly sick, but she needed some attention. I explained to the young mother that the dog needed some medication and I left her a small box full of yellow coated pills.

The postcard she sent me read: "Dear Dr. Green, The baby knocked the dog pills off the table and ate them. Will you please send me more for the dog?"

I stopped by Dee Walker's filling station late in the afternoon and Dee said that the Hess Ranch had been callin' me. I got Mr. Hill on the phone. He said that he had been out in the pasture and brought in a band of mares and colts and abscesses similar to those of the young stud were forming on several of these mares. Hill felt that we were in real trouble and asked that I come out as soon as I could.

The Hess Ranch was a sixty-mile call, which was common in my practice. Since it was summertime, it would get dark late and I needed to see these horses in some daylight, so I set up straight and spurred hard and drove into the Hess Ranch a little before sundown.

The young stud showed some slight improvement from his treatment, but nowhere near the miraculous recovery I had been getting from penicillin in my general practice. The mares in this band were good kinds of range brood mares. All of them had been broken at one time or another, and when one was roped out of the herd, she would turn and lead out, instead of fightin' and chokin' down like so many unbroken brood mares in the country would usually do.

As I examined them, I knew that they were suffering from the same thing as the young stud, and it was either contagious or infectious. It had to be some kind of an isolatable bug or a virus, and viruses in that part of the high, dry mountain country, especially during drouth, were almost unknown.

Such infections cause horses to lose weight even though they are being cared for, and these horses were showing such signs of unthrifty condition as bad hair and listlessness, but still weren't running high temperatures.

One of the oldest and most reliable treatments for bloodstream infections in horses is Fowler's Solution of Arsenic, and for want of a better medicine or a more accurate diagnosis, I resorted to drenching the affected mares by mouth and we finished the last mare after it was good dark.

I gave the little stud some more of that precious penicillin and decided that I would lance the abscess on his hip bone and pack it with another one of the recently discovered miracle drugs, sulfanilamide, which had only been out a few years. This I did very carefully by shaving the abscessed area before I lanced it. After I packed it with sulfanilamide, I sutured the incision and was careful to leave proper drainage at the bottom. Hill said he would keep the mares in a small pasture close to the headquarters and I told him I would look at them again sometime tomorrow.

When I got back to the office that night, I decided I had better do some research—the book kind. I had never learned all there was to know from my library and I was a practitioner who constantly referred to the writings of recognized authorities in the field of veterinary medicine. It was true that there were few or no sources of information concerning the toxic plantlife of the desert, but in a case such as the Hess horses, I felt that I must be confronted with some form of infection that science had dealt with and so I read until about two o'clock. When I began to nod, I decided I would go to bed and dream about them damned abscesses instead of readin' about 'em, and sure enough, I did.

I got back to the Hess horses the next day in the early afternoon and some of the baby colts had begun to show some slight swelling around their flanks and under their forearms. These were locations on the body where the grown horses had not seemed to develop any enlargements.

There was a good blood bay mare that had developed her first abscess on her shoulder point and I suddenly had the bright idea that maybe the pus from one of these abscesses would yield something that I had not been able to discover in blood samples, so I very carefully prepared a spot in the center of that abscess. I sterilized the external area, hoping that I would not pick up any airborne organisms that the mare might have on her hair or skin. When I lanced this abscess, I carefully got 50-cc. of pus in a sterile vial and quickly stoppered it and headed for the laboratory.

By this time, Mr. Hess had come out from San Antonio because he was seriously concerned about his horses and was pondering the possibility that this infection might be picked up by the cattle on the ranch. I told Mr. Hess frankly that up to this point I was baffled as to what type of infection we were dealing with and therefore I did not know whether or how it might spread. I had never met Mr. Hess before, but I found him to be an understanding and cooperative gentleman. He assured me that he was interested in solving the problem and was grateful for my conscientious concern. I rarely had this kind of conversation and I hardly knew how to thank him.

I decided to try several different lab techniques on this fresh pus. I made several slides with various kinds of stain, and at about dark I picked up a beautiful little round-shaped bug with a tail on him. After going through all my lab manuals, I identified the little culprit as being a rare type of protozoa. I started going through my books on *materia medica* to see what medical agent was indicated for the treatment of the protozoa. As I would read the description of the bug, each reference would wind up with "no known treatment."

Early next morning I went back to the Hess Ranch and explained to Mr. Hess and Mr. Hill what I had found out. While we talked about the problem, a Mexican cowboy spoke up and said that this was the "disease of the deer," that there were some dead deer in the mountains and others were doing very poorly. After we saddled some horses, Mr. Hill and I rode out the mountain pasture where the mares had been and we found several deer carcasses.

After further research in both my laboratory and my library, after phone calls to smarter men and to distant points, and more trips to the mountains, I finally proved that this type of protozoa could lay dormant in the crevices of rocks on the south side of the mountains in the warmth of sunlight for several years. In times of drouth when deer and other livestock would graze the steepest areas hunting vegetation that might grow from the moisture that ran off rocks, they would pick up the protozoa by mouth. There had been numerous cases of abscesses in wild deer that had been observed before, but the case of the Hess horses was to my knowledge the first protozoan infection of domestic range horses.

The stallion recovered without any after effects, but I always wondered how much good the penicillin did. However, any pus pocket that I packed with sulfanilamide would heal much faster than those that weren't treated, and the mares that we drenched several times with Fowler's Solution of Arsenic showed an even more rapid rate of recovery. However, this could have been from the desirable tonic effects of the arsenic, and I have always doubted that the arsenic treatment actually destroyed any protozoa.

The mares were moved into a better pasture and the cattle were taken out of the pasture where the deer were found and no abscesses ever appeared on the cattle. However, there is a reason that the cattle did not pick up the infection.

Deer by reason of the construction of a cleft in their upper lip can move either side of the lip separately, which enables them to pick up and move very short vegetation growth into their mouths and makes it possible for them to eat almost any grass or weeds that are visible above the ground.

Cattle do not have a cleft in their upper lip and they move the whole lip up and down from one side to the other at the same time with very little maneuverability. Since a cow doesn't have upper teeth in front, vegetation is brought into the mouth by sticking the tongue out and bringing the grass or weeds down against the lower teeth. Then the cow moves her head in an upward position to bite off the vegetation. In this respect the eating process of a cow is somewhat a handicap where sparse vegetation is concerned, and it probably was not possible for the cattle to have picked up the infection by mouth. Also, cattle are not inclined to graze and range in steep areas as much as wild game and horses are.

I really believe that the good summer rain that finally came in a very small mountain range probably did more to stop the infection than the research or treatment.

I had been in Old Mexico for a few days on business and came back by way of El Paso. I was sittin' in the Del Norte Hotel dining room with Buck Pyle when he went to answer the phone. I got up to leave and a man stopped me. He introduced himself as Mr. Doyle and said he ranched in southern Arizona near Wilcox. He said that he had heard something about my work on range poisons and told me that he was having some trouble on his range that he had never before experienced. He went on to say that he was running steer yearlings in some big pastures, and in one pasture he was losing a yearling or two every week and in the others none appeared to be sick. He said that he had had them vaccinated for blackleg and evidently that hadn't helped any, and he had had several vets out, but none of them had worked on the case long enough to find out anything.

He went on to say that a yearling or two a week was pretty expensive but he thought he could afford my services for at least a few days if I would care to make that long a trip. We made arrangements for me to meet him in Wilcox the next afternoon and go to look at his cattle and country.

As we drove to the ranch the next day, he went into more detail about moving these cattle in from Old Mexico. He had had some early rains and his range was good, and since he had kept yearlings on this pasture for a number of years, he was puzzled as to what could be different about vegetation or the cattle.

Driving around in his pickup, we saw a lot of cattle that appeared to be all right. We drove up to a windmill and one of the ranch cowboys rode up to water his horse and get a drink. While we were talkin', he volunteered the information that there was a yearling about two miles from there, as he pointed across the pasture, that was down. He said that from the signs of struggle on the ground, the yearling had been down for a day or two. After he had found him, he didn't know what to do but to report back to the headquarters, and he was glad that he had run onto us.

He loped ahead on his horse and took us to the yearling. I had brought along a small bag of instruments from my car just in case something like this came up. This yearling was in the last stages of the death struggle and was in an ideal condition to do a post-mortem. The liver, spleen, and kidneys showed a lot of chemical poisoning, and there was much discoloration in the stomach and intestinal tract.

Since this was a range steer receiving no supplementary feed, the presence of chemical poisoning struck me as being very odd. I asked Mr. Doyle about pipelines, oil wells, gas lines, and any other type of mineral or chemical presence that I could think of. None of these rang a bell with him or the cowboy.

We were driving back along the pasture road with lots of scenery and no conversation when I noticed a draw that was a solid patch of brown for a mile or so; it was a sudden contrast to the green vegetation around it. I asked him to stop the pickup. When I pointed to the brown patch, you could see the expression on his face change as it dawned on him that he had forgotten to tell me that these weeds had been sprayed with chemical weed poison.

He told me all about spraying the thistle in that draw in order to try to get rid of it; this was the only place on the ranch that any of it grew. He went on to explain that the spray was guaranteed to be completely harmless to all livestock.

Well, in my practice, I had discarded years back the idea that any chemical was completely harmless, so we drove over into the middle of this brown patch of weeds. There were tender green weeds and grass coming up underneath the taller growth that had been killed with spray. Any cattle grazing the younger growth would have to eat some of the dead weed along with each mouthful of green feed.

We drove back to the ranch headquarters and I asked to see the spraying machine. It was a good, clean, well-kept machine with no corrosion inside the tank. It seemed that this was going to be another case of being a detective instead of a doctor. I asked him where the containers that the chemical came in were. He said that he bought so much of it that he had asked for a fifty-five-gallon drum because of the savings in price.

We went into the back of a shed where the empty drum was kept. This iron drum lacked being empty by about one and a half inches of brown juicy stuff in the bottom. As I reached over to tilt it and shake that brown juice around, the iron drum came apart and the bottom fell out and that dab of brown stuff poured out onto the ground. It had eaten the bottom of the drum out.

I caught about half a pint in a glass jar before it all got away and told Mr. Doyle that we had probably found the trouble. He began to repeat how harmless this spray was and how many other people he knew had used it without any ill effects.

I told him I thought we ought to talk to the dealer who sold him this spray, and he said he bought it from a ranch-supply company at Safford, Arizona. I didn't think that I would have to come back to this ranch, so I drove over to Safford in my car and he went in his.

The man at the ranch-supply company was very cordial and glad to see us at first, and evidently hadn't heard about the yearlings that had been dying. He opened the conversation by asking Mr. Doyle the kind of results he had gotten on the weeds that he sprayed. Before Mr. Doyle could answer, he began to tell what good results everyone else had gotten from that spray.

I asked if I could see a can of the concentrated spray that they had been using on the weeds. He turned around and pointed to a bright five-gallon can, and I walked over and began readin' the label. I wasn't exactly tryin' to trap the man, but I needed more information, so I asked: "Was the same label on the fifty-five-gallon drum that you sold Mr. Doyle?"

He hastened to explain that Mr. Doyle was the only customer who wanted a fifty-five-gallon drum and they had emptied enough cans to fill up a drum, then delivered it to him at drum prices. I asked him if he had such an empty can around. By this time he had begun to get a little bit cagy and asked me "Why?" I said I wanted to see if the can was lined.

He was beginning to look pretty serious and he said that he had never thought about whether or not they were lined. He said further that the company had been giving credit for returned empty cans, and he had wondered why they were valuable.

Mr. Doyle said, "I've lost some cattle and if you've got an empty can, I want him to see it."

He shuffled around in the back of the store and came up with a can that had been returned for credit. I held the can up to the light and peeped through that small hole in the top; there seemed to be a lining or interior coating of some kind in the can.

We took a heavy pair of tin cutters, cut the can open and, with little effort, slipped a plastic liner loose from the inside of the container. The ranch-supply man was very much ill at ease, and Mr. Doyle was on the verge of getting mad.

He and I walked away and talked awhile, and I asked him if he thought it would be necessary for me to do any more research on the case. He told me that he owed the ranch-supply company enough to be able to get a settlement before he paid his bill and he felt that he didn't need any more information. However, in the event that the case should come to trial, he would have me subpoenaed, and I knew this would entitle me to reasonable pay and mileage.

While we were talking he asked, "How much do I owe you for this call?"

I told him what my fee would be, and instead of giving me a check on the ranch-supply company, like most people would, he said, "Go on back to your car, and I'll go back in the office and get your check for you now."

I don't know what this little settlement cost the ranch-supply company, but I imagine that the price of steer yearlings broke them of the habit of saving cans for return credit.

RABIES

About two o'clock one hot July afternoon, I was sittin' on the south porch of my office lookin' out across the desert, watchin' the heat waves rise up from the rock and sand and play on the scrub growth of greasewood and black brush that made their leaves and limbs appear to be movin', when an excited young mother of three slid the tires and kicked up the dust in front of the office and called to me in an excited tone of voice. I stepped down from the screened porch and pulled my hat down to shade my eyes from the glaring sun and she immediately started on her story.

She had a nice big collie dog in her backyard and one of the children had had a little fever. She had called Dr. Oswald and as he walked through the fenced yard to the house, he saw the big dog lying in the cool drip next to the house under the air conditioner. After he checked the baby's fever and talked to the mother awhile, he said, "I believe that dog out in the front yard has rabies. Have these children been playing with him?"

She almost went into a panic as she said, "Heavens, yes! They all play with him." Then she had dashed from her house to my office to ask me to come and destroy the dog.

In times of drouth, when the natural feed for foxes, wolves, coons, skunks, and other small animals of prey get scarce, they will change their eating habits and will consume whatever can be found around the edges of civilization. It was not uncommon at this stage of a drouth to see foxes come into town at night to prowl the garbage cans. Other wild animals that weren't so easily seen moved into town and to ranch headquarters to the feed and water troughs that were kept full for the livestock.

This concentration of wildlife will cause enough exposure to the skunk population, which is the principal parent host of the Negri rabies infection. It seems that dogs, wolves, and foxes are the most readily bitten species that will transmit the rabies to domestic animals and man.

The Edwards Plateau and the Trans-Pecos Region was practically all net wire fence and sheep ranches, and the ranchers and government trappers had had drives and had trapped and killed wolves until there were no more left in the country. This left the transmission of the disease to domestic animals to the foxes, dogs and skunks.

There had been considerable talk about some isolated cases of rabies in foxes that had been killed. Their heads were sent to the state laboratory in Austin, but no cases had been diagnosed in any other livestock at the time this episode broke out in the yard from the sudden diagnosis of a medical doctor.

I followed the woman back to her house in my car, and as we came into the yard, the old dog looked up from his shady place and wagged his tail. She rushed into the house and stood behind the screen door and told me not to take any chances of him bitin' me too. As I got to within about four feet of the dog, the odor I smelled was a common one any practitioner could recognize.

As I rubbed this beautiful collie dog on the head, I noticed that his hair was bad. When I opened his mouth, I saw the lesions and sluffing that were causing the slobbering that Dr. Oswald had mistaken for rabies; he had a very advanced case of sore mouth and it could not have been taken for rabies by any person who was familiar with the disease. I turned to the woman and told her that she had fed this dog on either dry or canned commercial dog food and he had not been getting any fresh meat, that he was suffering from a dietary insufficiency, which I could cure by injections.

She was trembling and her voice was shaky, and she said she couldn't possibly take the chance with her children.

She told me to destroy the dog right there or take him with me. She said that she wanted his head sent to the laboratory at Austin the fastest possible way and that expense was secondary. This was an old dog. His teeth were bad but there was no good reason for destroying the faithful family pet. I tried to talk her out of it but had no success.

I put the dog in the back of my car and took him to my office. Now, I never prided myself on being a small-animal doctor and did not want to encourage any small-animal practice, but at the same time I felt it my professional duty not to start a hysterical epidemic of rabies in the human mind, which is the most damaging.

My first inclination was to save the old dog and I was reasonably sure that I could, but I would have half the mothers in town on me by morning if I didn't get that head on the way to Austin. Since this was an old dog whose days of usefulness were about spent, I very painlessly did away with him and very expertly severed his head.

To be sure that I had the proof and evidence in the proper place, I carried the head up to Dr. Oswald's with the usual containers and ice necessary to pack a rabies specimen for shipment. On the front porch of his office, I had him watch me put the head in a dry metal container and then put that container in a larger metal bucket and pack ice all around it. I very carefully sealed both buckets and had his secretary address the package to the state laboratory in Austin. I said to Ozzie, "Let's go put this on the airplane"—which was to leave Fort Stockton airport in a matter of minutes—"and then stop somewhere and get some coffee."

I had concealed my feelings and he thought that this was a social visit, so he watched the bucket being loaded on the plane without suspecting that I was building a case.

It was then about four o'clock, and from that time until

midnight I had twenty-three calls from all parts of the surrounding country asking about the rabies epidemic. I said that I didn't know we were in a rabies epidemic, but I knew if we were, it would have to be from some other source than that old sore-mouth dog that spent his life in the yard playing with babies and living on a deficient diet.

At eleven o'clock the next morning I got a wire from the state laboratory stating that there was no evidence of rabies and the head was negative. I took the wire by to show the mother of the little children. She was rather silent about the affair and by now was in better control of her emotions.

Then I went to Dr. Oswald's office and waited until he wasn't busy and, in the presence of his secretary, I gave him a damn strong cussin' for practicin' veterinary medicine and for exciting an epidemic. But the word was already on the wind and the horror of human hydrophobia was already vividly pictured in the minds of the nervous, excitable intellectuals and the stupid, superstitious of the population. By dark that day I had vaccinated forty-seven dogs and three house cats for rabies, and I wired the laboratory in Kansas City to send me another three hundred doses of rabies vaccine.

I was careful in conversation over the phone and in talking to people who were concerned about the seriousness of the disease. At no time did I discourage anyone from having an animal of any species vaccinated, and since the vaccine itself had reached a high state of perfection and there was less than one half of one per cent breaks in vaccination, it clearly showed that mankind had made tremendous progress with the disease since the nineteenth century when Louis Pasteur vaccinated himself with the first effective treatment and proved by risking his own life that there was hope for a human being bitten by a rabid animal and that mankind could take steps to protect the domestic animal from rabies.

The mayor of McCamey called me that night and asked if I could come to McCamey early the next morning—all the dogs, cats, and other pets were being brought to the city hall, where he wanted me to vaccinate them. I had enough vaccine on hand to carry me through the McCamey scare, and as I drove back to Fort Stockton I realized that the vaccine I had ordered from Kansas City could not have arrived yet, and I expected to be behind with my treatments by morning.

There were some people with dogs at my office when I got in that night, and I explained to them that I would get fresh vaccine by plane the next day. The plane landed at eleven fifteen and by one o'clock I was again vaccinating dogs at my office.

About midafternoon, I received a call from an oilfield driller at Grand Falls, about forty miles north of Fort Stockton. He said he had a cow that a mad dog must have bitten and she was slobbering at the mouth and falling into the fence; he wanted to know how quickly I could get there.

Cattle and horses are subject to two different forms of rabies. "Mute" rabies is manifested by an animal who stands quietly with his jaws open and can't swallow, but in most cases he is not wild or excited and is no trouble to handle. Mute rabies could easily be mistaken in a cow for a case of a bone or a stick hung in the throat, and mute rabies in a horse could also be mistaken for some mouth or throat trouble.

There are known cases where a stockman has stuck a hand and arm into the jaw of a rabid cow and contracted rabies and died because of some slight scratch or open wound on his hand. In one such case a dairyman had been conscious and had been able to give instructions to kill the rabid cow.

The symptoms of rabies as they appear in other animals is commonly referred to as "active" rabies in horses and cattle, and the behavior of such affected animals is characterized by extreme nervousness. They will rub huge patches of hide off their shoulders and legs, and both cattle and horses will bite their forelegs and their sides. An active case of rabies in a cow will cause her to fight and run headlong into fences and anything else in sight. Horses are rarely known to paw with their forefeet but will kick at the slightest motion or touch from behind, and there have been cases in veterinary medicine where horses and mules have actually chased people and bit at them as slobbers flowed from their mouth.

When a human has been bitten by a rabid animal, there is only one thing that can and must be done: vaccination should be started as soon as possible and never later than five days after the person is bitten. This treatment consists of fourteen separate injections given every other day in the muscles of the belly wall; they are extremely painful and many times cause such side effects as nausea and other discomforts.

When I drove up to the oil driller's place at Grandfalls, they had the cow in a high corral fence made out of railroad crossties stuck in the ground that stood side by side and were tied to an iron pipe at the top, and this made it a big, stout fence. A crowd of people had gathered and were peepin' through the cracks at this "hydrophobic" cow. Nobody wanted to take the chance of opening the gate, so I crawled over it.

As I crawled over the gate and saw the cow slobbering, I knew it could not be a case of mute rabies and that I needed to look for the other symptoms of active rabies besides slobbering. She was a half-breed brindle Jersey cow that might weigh seven hundred pounds. She was extremely thin and her eyes were set, so to speak, in her head like an animal that is going to die, and streams of slobbers were pouring from her mouth.

Nobody offered to come in and help, but in my experience I had never seen a cow with active rabies in this seemingly far advanced stage of slobbers that had not rubbed the hair off her sides and shoulders and did not offer to bite the fence or bite her foreleg or gnaw at her side, and this cow apparently hadn't knocked a hair off from any nervous irritation.

I pitched a rope around her horns and threw the end of it over the fence so that some of the fellows who were watchin' could draw her head up to a post and tie her. I wasn't too scared, but I thought I ought to have her tied down even though in my opinion there was no evidence of rabies.

I took another lariat rope and slipped it around her hind legs, and since her head was tied to the fence, some of my audience got brave and came in to help me pull her hind legs out from under her. This would lay her flat on the ground on her side, so I could tell more about her mouth.

I went to the car and put on some rubber gloves and got a probing instrument about eighteen inches long and a wooden axhandle that I carried for such cases as this. I stuck the flat end of the axhandle in the side of the cow's mouth and then turned it to where it would hold her mouth open about four inches wide.

I very carefully and gently began to feel with the probing instrument for some swelling or foreign object in the back of her mouth and the upper part of her throat. You learn to almost have eyes at the ends of your fingers in the practice of veterinary medicine, and as I felt around, I found no hard object and an enlargement that I was pressing on didn't give to the pressure sufficiently to have been in the flesh.

I lifted her head up with another short piece of wood into a position where I could see down in her mouth. I detected something green, and with rubber gloves on I went behind the axhandle just a short way into the jaw I took a hold of a huge flat leaf of a prickly pear cactus that was imbedded and held in place by the spines of the cactus and jerked it out of her mouth and thereby "cured" another case of rabies.

Most of the people in the ranching regions of the Far Southwest didn't have telephones, and many times trips to the nearest telephone were almost as long as trips to town. One rancher who lived in the Davis Mountain region sent his wife about twenty miles to phone me to come see about a sick horse. She was unable to get me on the phone, so she went another twenty miles and that ranch's phone was out of order. Then she drove on into Fort Stockton, which made it about a sixty-five-mile trip.

The peculiarity of this horse's sickness was what kept driving her when she couldn't reach me and the phones didn't work. Her husband had told her that the horse was acting peculiar, and he thought that he had been bitten by a mad fox. The possibility of more livestock and the family pets being in danger had caused the rancher's wife to come in at a pretty reckless speed.

It was about noon, and when I started to say I would be out there after dinner, she said, "No, you won't. I'll beat you back and we'll have dinner after you've seen this sick horse that J. C. is so worried about."

When she took off in a cloud of dust, I had no doubt that she would beat me to the ranch because I wasn't that excited or in that big a hurry. I went by the drugstore and left word where I was going in case somebody else looked for me.

It was high noon when I drove up to the corral where all the ranch hands and some of the neighbors stood watchin' a good-lookin' dapple grey horse that was standing in the middle of the corral close to a water trough with his feet all spraddled out. This was a narrow water trough about twenty feet long, the top of which was eighteen inches from the ground so that sheep, cattle, and horses could all drink out of it.

We had a few howdys as I walked into the corral and J. C. told me that if I didn't think it was safe to go near the horse, not to take any chances. The horse could see the water at the top of the trough and he was standin' with his nose about two feet from the edge of the trough suckin' and makin' all the motions and noises of a horse drinkin' without knowin' that he didn't have his mouth in the water.

I asked one of the cowboys to pitch me a lariat rope and I walked up to the horse and slipped the rope over his head. When I tried to lead him, he ran backward as though he was goin' to choke and I gave him slack. One of the cowboys spoke up and said, "He's mad if I ever saw a mad horse, and as many dead foxes as there is in the mountains and around the water troughs, he could've sure been bit by one."

I didn't let his palaver bother me too much, and by rubbing around on the horse's head, I finally got his attention so that his eyes weren't so badly fixed on the ground, and in a few minutes he led up on a loose rope.

I saw some loose boards lying against the bottom of the fence and told J. C. to lay one of those boards across the open gate, which he did, and as I stepped over the board and the horse saw it, he ran backward the full length of the rope.

I asked how long they had been riding this horse. J. C. said that he was just an average kind of horse and they only used him for an extra and he had been runnin' out all summer until just a few days ago. I said, "You've been pasturin' your extra horses over there at the foot of the mountains, and the runoff from those little summer flash floods we've had in the mountains has caused some loco-weed to come in the flats, and this horse has a fair case of loco. When you rode him yesterday, you got him hot and 'brought it out' on him, so to speak, and he hasn't been bit by a rabid fox."

This brought on some volunteer talk from the cowboys who had been riding the other extra horses that were brought in with his horse, and they had seen signs of boogerin' and fright from common objects in their horses since they had been riding them the last few days.

Loco is a weed that grows in the semi-arid regions of the Southwest. The early summer growth of loco, which is tender, is readily eaten by horses and it affects their nervous systems and causes them to be more apt to shy from man-made objects. After a horse has apparently recovered from the symptoms, he may still show signs of nerve damage when he is ridden or worked and after he is hot. Most apparently gentle horses won't step over a rope or cross a plank laying in their pathway and are inclined to booger from almost any kind of a shadow on the ground.

When a horse has eaten as much as 30 per cent of his body weight in loco over a period of time, he will develop extreme nervousness, stagger when he tries to move, and will continue to lose coordination through a prolonged ill-ness until he dies. This dapple grey horse was an in-between case: he had too much loco to be useful but not enough to kill him; and if he should recover sufficiently to be used again, he would still do things that would cause him to be referred to as locoed.

J. C.'s wife, true to her word, had a big dinner on the table by the time we finished with the horse. At the dinner table lots of hearsay rabies stories were told by the cowboys. After dinner, I vaccinated the family pets, dogs, and cats and went back to town.

I was in the back of the drugstore talking to Roger Gallemore when Blanche came through the front door in a loud pair of shorts and pullin' on a long cigarette and callin' to me in a loud tone of voice. In a tone that easily could have been heard all over town, she went to tellin' me that there was something bad wrong with her Pekingese house dog; it was actin' strange and she just knew it was about to go mad.

I had vaccinated this Pekingese dog at six-month intervals for about three years, and I knew there was no possible chance that it had rabies. When she lowered her tone of voice and started blowin' her cigarette smoke, I told her that the only possible way that her house dog could be takin' rabies was that she had bitten some of the children and some of the children had bitten the dog. She left the store cussin' me, and said that as crazy as I was gettin' I must have been bit by some'n myself. This was the kind of thing that made me popular.

I had eaten a big dinner and was lyin' on a pallet on the porch when Rafael rode up on a mule, bareback with a blind bridle on him. He said, "Dok-tor, I theenk my other mule ees sick in the head. I hate veery much to disturb you from your siesta, but we must do something for my mule."

Rafael lived about two miles out of town on an irrigated farm, and I told him to head back home on his mule and I would be there in a few minutes. I waited long enough for Rafael to get home on his mule, and I drove up at about the same time that he got to the mule corral.

There was a nice little three-sided 'dobe barn with a loft in it that opened out to the south. Rafael's mules were the small, good kind of little Mexican mule and were well broke and gentle. The corral fence had been grown by planting yuccateae cactus close together and training the branches across each other. It was a very typical desert fence, really a wall of cactus thorns, and would sure hold any kind of livestock.

The little mule had run and fallen into the fence and had cactus stickers all over one shoulder, and from the time Rafael had left home until the time we got back to the corral, he had rubbed that shoulder raw on the front post of the barn. Rafael was very excited and his wife and several young children had been standin' outside the fence and hollerin' and chunkin' the mule to try to get him to stop rubbin'.

The little mule was slobbering at the mouth and had a wild look in his eyes. When a small spotted Spanish goat started across the corral, he ran at him and picked him up in his mouth by the neck and shook him like a dog would shake a rabbit. Rafael started through the gate with a garden hoe to beat him off the goat. I pulled him back and shut the gate and explained to him that the mule had the disease of the "mad-dog bite."

He turned and, in a high tone of voice, told his wife and children in Spanish to go back to "la casa." I was explaining that rabies was caused by the bite of a skunk or dog or some such animal when he began to wave his hands in the air. He took off his hat and whipped his legs and burst into a fit of Spanish that was akin to an unknown tongue.

When he finally got control of himself, he explained to me that there had been a momma skunk with some kittens in the hay in the loft of the barn and that they were "mucho bonito" and that he and the children had watched them. About two weeks ago he had seen the momma skunk come down out of the loft into the feed trough where the mule was eating and bite the mule on the nose. The mule had snorted and whirled out of the corral and slung the skunk loose from his nose and Rafael said, "You know sometheeng else, that skunk and those kittens have disappeared since that day."

I went to the car and got a .30-.30 rifle and shot the mule through the heart. You never shoot a rabid animal through the head if you might want to send it off, because you would damage the brain.

I explained to Rafael about sending the head to Austin, and he said that the presence of the skunk, the word of me, the Dok-tor, and how the mule acted was all the proof that he needed. I cautioned him that he must kill the goat and burn or bury it, and he said that he would do that when he dragged the mule off.

This was the only case of rabies that occurred in a domestic animal during this several weeks' rabies scare, and it was caused by the bite of the skunk. It would be hard to estimate the true benefit that was derived from the extensive vaccination campaign that was brought about by this scare, and the circumstances may have prevented an outbreak of rabies in domestic dogs.

The fox by nature is a coward and relies on his cunning for survival and not on his ability as a fighter. In his rabid condition when he started into civilization in his subconscious state he was still not a fighter. I seriously doubt that the foxes that were dying over the country ever bit any domestic livestock. And so, the worst part of the so-called rabies epidemic was in the human mind.

HORMONES

In my early years in Fort Stockton more ranchers tried grazing sheep on irrigated fields, and due to the war, everybody wanted to produce as much livestock as possible on the acres involved. Considerable interest had been manifested in the possibility of treating ewes to cause them to bring two lambs a year. Hormone therapy was something which had been talked about in the livestock industry but on which very little research had been done. Little knowledge was available pertaining to the treatment of domestic animals with hormones.

I wrote several laboratories that I thought might have information that had not been released, but their response was disappointing, and what information they had to offer did not apply to range conditions.

I began my first attempt to develop a satisfactory hormone preparation by using hormones in injectable form that were compounded in sesame oil. I injected four different pens of ten ewes each. These sheep were all of the same breeding and age. Two pens were injected with two different natural hormones; the third pen was injected with an artificial chemical hormone; and the fourth pen with a blended hormone.

One of these pens of ewes that were treated with artificial hormones became highly nervous and went off their feed and drank unusual amounts of water. Some of them got in bad enough condition to make me think that they might die, so I "posted" one of these ewes and found that the artificial hormone had had a very harsh effect on the reproductive organs of the sheep and had caused severe hemorrhage in the ovaries and extreme contractions in the tubes of the reproductive organs.

Another pen of ten ewes that were treated with pure estrogenic hormones showed little or no reaction and gave no indications of being ready to breed. Since these ewes were doing exceptionally well and were fat, we slaughtered one for mutton and I examined the reproductive organs. There had not been even a slight reaction. Repeated treatment on these ewes with natural estrogen finally caused them to breed, but the repeated treatments would have been too expensive and too time-consuming to be practical.

The ten ewes that were treated with blended hormones produced a false cycle and in a few days (three to seven days) had a reoccurring fertile cycle and we turned the bucks in. When I determined that these ewes were all with lamb, I treated fifty ewes with the same blend and turned them out under range conditions. These fifty ewes produced forty-eight lambs, which is 96 per cent, and the ten ewes that had been kept in a small lot on feed produced twelve lambs, two of them having twins, which is 120 per cent.

All these sheep were dry ewes that had missed a spring lamb and had been cut out from the main herd at shearing time, and they produced lambs in the early winter and were grazed on irrigated fields. These ewes all showed some age and were broken-mouthed and normally would have been sent to market in the summer after they were sheared. Their lambs weighed around ninety pounds at Easter marketing time and the ewes were also fat and could be shipped with the lambs. This was a good trick in that it got a lamb from an old ewe at an ideal time of year and she was still marketable without any loss from having produced this last lamb.

Dry ewes have always been a loss factor in range sheep, and these experiments pointed to the possibility of making a better market for old ewes that could be bred and grazed on irrigated fields and also on Panhandle wheat pastures.

The following year Othro Adams bought a good number of dry ewes out of the wool from a rancher in the Glass Mountains. He and I went out and "hormoned" these ewes and left them there a few weeks to breed up. This gave him time to cut some more irrigated alfalfa hay before he moved these ewes onto the fields to lamb and graze until time to ship to the Easter market. This would be about the right time to get livestock off the alfalfa to start another season of cutting hay.

My hormone research received wide acclaim. I named my blended product Ewetone and shipped it in large quantities to a number of states.

Young range sheep are hard to get a good percentage of

lambs from the first year that they are bred. Ranchers referred to breeding "yearling ewes," but, actually, these so-called yearling ewes were almost two years old, and under semi-arid range conditions, such young ewes rarely bred and produced more than a 60 per cent lamb crop the first year.

With little additional experimentation, the blended product Ewetone was being used on hundreds of thousands of young range ewes. After treatment, they produced from 85 to 100 per cent. Range ewes are bred to bring spring lambs, and treatment with Ewetone was not to change the lambing time but to increase the lambing percentage.

I produced the blended hormone product in a sesame-oil base in my laboratory and packaged it for small flocks in the Eastern states in 1-cc. ten-dose vials, and for the Western range-sheep trade, I packaged it in 50-cc. amber vials with hypodermic rubber stoppers. This was a very stable product and required no refrigeration or special handling and was easy to administer.

I was working in my laboratory when Cleo McKenzie, who had ranching interests scattered around but at that time had his main operation around Tunis Springs, came in and began to tell me about a horse that had a big knot "rise up" on his shoulder point. He said he had taken his knife and stuck the blade through a little piece of wood so it wouldn't go too deep into the knot on the shoulder of the horse, then he jobbed it right quick to open it, and the pus and corruption just flowed. He had taken his knife out of his pocket and was showing me about how thick the block of wood was on the blade and about how much of the blade was left that he used to open the knot. He went on to tell me that he had had to open it two or three times more, and he wondered if I could give him something to put on it.

This home practice was common among Western ranchers, and it was often necessary to overcome what had been done to the horse. I was fixin' him up a package of healing powders, and since I didn't want anything counteractin' these healing powders, I asked Cleo to let me see his knife again. He very unsuspectingly handed me his knife. With the other hand I handed him the healing powders and said, "You can have your knife back when the horse gets well."

As the drouth moved in and became more severe, the ranchers in the drouth area were constantly selling off the older ewes, and finally only the young ewes were left on the ranches. In one of the most severe years of drouth about three hundred thousand young ewes in the Trans-Pecos Region were treated with hormones to ensure a good lamb crop. There was no break in the sunshine, wind, and dry weather.

When sheep have baby lambs, they need to be in good enough condition that they come into their natural milk flow and have full bags, which causes them to claim their baby lambs. If a ewe is poor due to drouth or other conditions, she will have her lamb and then walk off and leave it. It seems that the instinct for survival is more pronounced than the mother instinct.

When lambing season started on these last treated ewes, the drouth had reached its worst stage, and these young mother sheep had their lambs on barren ranges with no grass or weeds and only dead brush to survive on, and most of the lamb crop was lost. For the next several years of the drouth no one was interested in treating what few sheep they had, and the sheep that they hung on to, hoping for rain, they didn't really care whether they brought a lamb crop or not.

Some of the mountain regions of New Mexico hadn't gotten quite as dry as the Trans-Pecos and I had begun to spread out, advertise, and travel some of that country and sell my hormone products for sheep and cattle. Cattle are much easier to get to breed and calve than sheep and there was the need in the range industry for a hormone product that could be used to cause cows to calve at a particular time of year, which would enable a rancher to make the best possible use of his range and have calves of uniform size at shipping time.

With the experience I had had in developing a hormone product for sheep, I took several short cuts in testing various blends of hormones in treating heifers of breeding age. After a few trial-and-error experiences, by the end of my first year of research, I had Cowtone ready for commercial use.

Breeding cattle does not present too much of a problem and the big advantage to be had by the use of Cowtone on heifers was in setting their calving time with the first calf and causing them all to calve within a short period—thus making calves uniform at the time of shipment the following fall. By starting heifers to breed at a particular time of year, with good range management as to when to put the bulls out on range and take them off, they could very well be controlled to calve at the same time of year for the rest of their productive life.

Bert Kincaid was back from service in the Second World War and was drenching sheep for intestinal parasites on a commercial custom basis. He and I had overlapping interests in the livestock medicine business that caused us to work together a good deal. In need of business and work, we began to solicit large herds of heifers in New Mexico of breeding age to treat with Cowtone. We made trips into Clovis, Fort Sumner, and on up into the mountain regions of New Mexico.

Bert was a big, stout young man with exceptionally good hands and arms, and he could inject as many sheep or cattle in a day as anyone I ever had help me. We also got along well with one another and our away-from-home business was getting us both enough money to enable us to do as our ranching friends were: hanging on until it rained and the country would be restocked.

I met Tobe Foster, who was a rancher, oil operator, and speculator in Lubbock, in the lobby of the St. Angelus Hotel in San Angelo. He was interested in having five thousand young ewes treated on his Block Ranch at Capitán, New Mexico, that fall to ensure a good lamb crop the following spring. Bert and I made definite plans to go up to Capitán, and Mr. Foster was to furnish all the labor to help us and have the sheep gathered and at the working pens on Monday of Thanksgiving week. This would be a big deal for Bert and me in the dead of winter when we had very little other business.

It was a hard day's drive from Fort Stockton to Capitán. Bert and I left about daylight Sunday morning, planning to get to Capitán on Sunday night, when we were to meet Tobe Foster. Monday passed and Tobe Foster didn't show up, and we were unable to get him by phone in Lubbock.

We finally drove out to the ranch and talked to the foreman. He hadn't heard anything about the hormoning of the sheep, but he said that this sort of slipshod arrangement wasn't too uncommon with Foster, and he didn't doubt our story and would take his ranch hands and gather sheep all day Tuesday, and we could come back Wednesday morning and go to work.

The weather was unsettled but not bad. Bert and I found time to pass pretty slow around Capitán, where there were only two or three general stores and Pearl's Café. We drove over to Carrizozo without running into any excitement and came back to Capitán, where we were staying in a rooming-house type of hotel.

The weather took a turn for the worse during the night and about eighteen inches of snow fell by morning, and the temperature dropped to 5 degrees above. When we started to the ranch, we followed a snow plow out of town to the turn-off, which was about ten miles from the ranch head-quarters. We managed to make it through the snow over a ranch road to the headquarters, where we changed our instruments and vials of hormones over into a jeep. We went about another fifteen miles across the ranch to where the first fifteen hundred ewes were bunched.

Several Indian sheepherders had built up a good fire behind the cedar breaks about a hundred yards from the corrals. Bert and I didn't tarry around the fire too long because we didn't want to get used to it if we were goin' to have to work in the snow and cold all day.

The Indians weren't too anxious to leave the fire to work the sheep, and when they got out and into the snow, we had trouble getting the Indians or the sheep to move and work into the chute. I noticed several old sheep hides on the fence, so I gathered them up and rolled them up in a bundle with the wool side showing and tied a wire to the bundle and drug it around through the sheep and tried to get them to follow it into the chute. They didn't shy or booger from the skins of their dead kinfolk, but they weren't interested in letting a bundle of dead hides act as a lead ram.

After this hide trick failed, Bert took a sheep by the head and drug it slowly through the snow and bleated like a sheep and got some of the others to start following. The dragging of the lead sheep and the tromping of the others that followed beat down the snow which had piled inside the chute fences so that the sheep couldn't step over the fence as they would have been able to do on snow.

This chute was a little too wide and we crowded in as many sheep as possible so they couldn't turn around in the chute. When we had them all headed the same way, they were about four sheep wide across the chute. Bert and I started working at the back of the chute hormoning two sheep apiece, using one hand to part the wool on the thick part of the hindquarter and using a three-quarter-inch 18-gauge needle to make the 1-cc. hormone injection. As we finished those four sheep, we stepped in front of them and pushed them back and took the next four. The chute would hold about fifty head and we were tellin' each other that we might get through before we froze to death.

The first slowdown that we weren't prepared for happened when the sesame oil got so thick from the cold that it couldn't be forced through the needles. We had to build up a fire close to the chute and lay the bottles of Ewetone close enough to the fire to keep warm; we changed bottles often to keep the oil thin enough to work. Another advantage we discovered about changing bottles from around the fire was that a warm bottle would help warm our cold hands for a few minutes before the oil got too thick to flow. Before long, Bert was doing the injecting and I was standing between him and the fire, passing the bottles both directions.

We went back to the fire where the Indian ranch hands were and tried to talk them into helping us, and their spokesman said, "Me can't see no hurry. Sheep be here all winter."

This tapped off my high temper, and I gave him a fair cussin' and asked him why he didn't go back to the headquarters. He said, "Indian no walk in snow. Wait till jeep go back."

I could tell by the way he said it that he didn't think it would be very long before we froze out on the job. That Indian didn't know how much money Bert and I had tied up in hormones and in the trip.

Bert and I went back to work and after a while Bert began to tell me that his feet were frozen. I asked him how he could tell, and he said that they felt like it. I said, "Hell, they aren't frozen or you couldn't feel 'em. I know 'cause I can't feel mine."

This type of encouragin' conversation went on between us all day and there were a few times when we picked up a cold metal syringe and it would be so cold that it would stick to our hands.

We got through in the late afternoon and the Indians had gotten tired of waiting and had drifted away from the fire. We fired up the company jeep that had snow tires on it and started back to the headquarters. As we started off of a high ridge below a mountain road down into a deep gorge, I looked to one side and said, "Bert, where's that steam comin' from?"

We were traveling real slow and he stopped the jeep and said, "What steam?" About two hundred feet up a narrow canyon there was some white steam.

We got out of the jeep and walked over to the edge of this narrow gorge and there was what appeared to be about four hundred sheep that had found protection in the canyon, which was also dotted with scrub cedar. They were humped up and covered with snow and their breath and the heat of their bodies was making the steam that attracted my attention.

I said, "Bert, we are already frozen to death and at the most we have only used eighteen hundred doses of that five thousand contract. This bunch of sheep are humped up in a protected spot. Why don't we just ease among 'em and shoot 'em with some hormone."

"It's all right with me, but I don't think we can build a fire with the snow as deep as it is. How are we going to keep the hormone warm?"

"Leave the jeep runnin' and set the bottles around on the motor and radiator."

We pulled the jeep about as close as we thought was safe and started working these sheep. They weren't too bad off, as far as weather was concerned, and they were too smart to be scared out of their protection, so we walked among them and crowded them up against the canyon wall and by the cedar trees and started injecting them with hormone and doing our best to walk through them and keep the treated ones behind us. We may have given a few an extra shot or two to be sure we got 'em all.

About fifty feet from the end of the canyon, an Indian sheepherder dressed in plenty of warm clothes with a blanket over his head rolled out from under some cedar trees. He spoke plenty of English and was half-mad because we had loosened the sheep, so to speak, and pushed them back from the cedars where he had curled up. The cedar was knocking the snow off of him and the herd of sheep were thick enough around him that he had a warm spot to wait out the norther.

He told us he had started to the corral with these sheep the day before and in the late afternoon had herded them into that canyon for the night and the snow during the night made him stay in the canyon. I asked him if he had anything to eat and he explained that he had some tortillas and beans in a marrell. He had a cactus-fiber marrell slung over his shoulder under about half of his clothes that he showed me, and it looked like it was still about half full of grub, which would have been enough to have lasted an Indian sheepherder bedded up under a cedar thicket a week.

By now it was almost dark and we got in the jeep—we let the herder come with us—and drove into the headquarters for the night. There were other hands working on the ranch and there was a big, old, fat, filthy, nearsighted

Dutchman who was the ranch cook. As nasty as he looked and as greasy as his grub was, it was still pretty tasty after a day in the snow. Bert and I went to bed upstairs in a little room without any fire and not quite enough cover, but it was warmer than what we had had all day and we were so tired that we had to get warmer before we knew that we were cold and we made it pretty good till daylight.

It snowed some more durin' the night and the ranch foreman wasn't too interested in our project and all the ranch hands had quit work because of the weather, so Bert and me were holed up on Thanksgiving Day with seven or eight Indian-Mexican half-breeds and a fat, nasty cook. We had the fattest turkey and the greasiest dressing and the sweetest raisin pie that anybody ever tried to eat—and the most uninteresting conversation.

When we got through as much of this batch of stuff as we could stand, I told Bert that I believed that we could break through that bank of snow to civilization. He said, "I bet you can't get off without me."

We started down the mountain about two in the afternoon. We slid and pushed and took our chances and got out to the public road, where there had been a snow plow about five o'clock, and made it to Capitán just at dark. We had already had a batch of Capitán, so we decided to drive on to Roswell and spend the night. It was about seventy miles to Roswell and the town was crowded, and it was late in the night when we found a good old stone-wall hotel with a single room and a double bed and plenty of cover.

It had been a cold trip and when Bert started to pull his socks off that night, he found that they had frozen to his feet from pushing and working in the snow and then driving into town in a cold car. We missed Thanksgiving at home and had a pretty rough nonprofitable trip. We were glad that it was over and decided that we wouldn't answer any farflung calls in the mountains until spring.

I tried for several weeks to get Tobe Foster on the phone. I sent a bill to his office, and when the ewes were supposed to start lambing five months later, his accountant sent me a check for the trip.

PLOWS AND PROPELLERS

There's a few gadgets on this earth that I've tried to stay clear of. Two in particular that infested and disturbed the peace and tranquility of the Far Southwest were plows and propellers.

When I was a small boy playing on the floor, one of my bigger brothers dropped a geography book and I saw pictures in there where there hadn't been any of the earth turned over and it was still in grass. I had spent the most part of my life hunting country like that and had nearly found it when pumpkin rollers came from various parts of the world to drill wells, cut down good mesquite trees, and plow up grass to raise something that the government already had too much of and the market was bad.

The gadget that I had still less use for was the airplane. It has always been my heartfelt opinion that horseback in high country is high enough off the ground for me to be. Well, airplanes were gettin' to be too common and many ranchers in this farflung country had bladed out and graded up airstrips for them and their neighbors to use and a lot of ranchers were keeping some kind of fly-ships of their own. Whenever I walked into a crowd where the conversation was plows and propellers, I knew I didn't belong and stayed clear of that type of unpleasant conversation.

Othro Adams had a plane and was considered to be an excellent pilot by those who may have known. He had offered me some

very enticing propositions to fly over different flocks of
sheep for some reason or another and I had always turned
him down.

One morning a big, fat, gray-headed, past-middle-age man
walked into my office and introduced himself. We started
what seemed to me would be a nice visit. However, he
came to the point pretty fast. He ranched in northern
Arizona and grazed mostly steers that he bought and sold
every year. The more he talked about his ranch operation,
the more I knew he had made or stole his money in some
other industry, because his cow talk didn't fit together too
good.

The reason he had come to see me was that for several
weeks now they had been finding an occasional dead steer
in the mountains on his range. He said he was glad he
caught me when I wasn't busy because he had landed at
the Fort Stockton airfield and caught a car to town. His
pilot was at the Officers' Club at the airfield waiting for us
and he would fly me up to the ranch. After I saw his
cattle, if necessary, he would have me back home tonight.

I tried not to show any pangs of shock, but I wasn't
fixin' to fly to northern Arizona in that airship. I asked him
how many steers he had and he didn't exactly know but
thought there were between twenty-seven hundred and
three thousand head. This was sure proof that he wasn't
a cowman or he would've known within three head how
many had died and how many were livin'.

I told him I'd be glad to go look into his steer troubles
but that I had resented the encroachment of the automobile
earlier in life and still didn't like 'em and liked airplanes
even less, and it looked to me like he had enough cattle for
some of 'em to still be alive after I drove up there in my
car, which would take about two days.

Well, he thought this was ridiculous and had an awful

big laugh, then said, "Doc, surely you're joking." He went on to tell me how many millions of dollars' worth of business he tended to on the West Coast as well as the ranch because he was able to fly and save time. He started to recite to me all the miracles of modern medicine that were being performed because of the use of airplanes and I would have to come to the licklog and progress with the times or I would lose my practice.

I said, "You may know what you're talkin' about, but you're overlookin' my distaste for licklogs, and let me ask you how come you went to the trouble to come see me about your steers when there're good doctors in Flagstaff and Phoenix and Page and in other parts of Arizona?"

"Oh well, you know you got sort of a reputation for working on range conditions and I just thought I'd let 'ya take a look at my range and cattle."

"Well, I believe I'll let you take your little airship and go back home without me."

He kind of blowed off a batch of steam and jumped up out of his chair and said if he had known I was an old fogey, he would have saved himself a trip.

I walked up to the Stockton Pharmacy in a little while and George Baker, the newspaperman, Joe Henson, and three or four more had just heard this big ranch operator blow off a batch of his opinion about their village horse doctor. I'm sure none of them spoke up to defend me, but it had struck them funny that he thought that he had unnerved me by his visit.

Four or five days later I got a call about dark from the big operator and flyboy from Arizona. He said that they had rounded up the steers on a part of the ranch and the cowboys told him that some more had died.

After he thought his and my visit over, he had decided that everybody had a right to their own way of travel and if I didn't want to ride in his $115,000 airplane, that was my business, and he would be glad to pay for the trip and my services if I would come to the ranch and look at his cattle. I told him I would be there the next afternoon in time to do some good. It was about a thousand-mile trip and he bellered over the phone, "Hell, you just as well have flown."

I drove into Jacob's Lake about two hours before sundown the next day and his ranch foreman met me and we headed still farther up into the mountains.

They were loose herding and allowing a herd of about five hundred head of steers to graze along a draw. Most of these cattle were in good flesh, but some of them were wobbly in their gait and the control and handling of their head and the rest of their body showed bad coordination. It was easy to tell that this was not loco, and since these cattle had not been fed any sort of commercial feed, it was unlikely that there was any fermentation condition existing that would have caused their sickness and death.

I rode the range all the next day horseback and pulled up and gathered about twenty different plants that I was suspicious of being in some stage of poison. Any desert plants and plants in other regions of the world contain acids or other toxic substances only at certain growing seasons or at certain stages of development. Many times weeds and grasses that are for the most part nutritious and even fattening can be toxic for a matter of a few days or a few weeks during a year's growth, and I was hoping that maybe this would be a case of that sort.

It was late spring in northern Arizona and the snow had melted and gone into the ground and caused some fair grazing to be available in the high mountain region. However, the drouth was reaching that direction and there had been no spring rains.

I never did quite figure out how many different rackets this old flyboy was making money out of on the West Coast, but he did have a palacious ranch headquarters. They were brushin' and curryin' and carryin' on over me and about the third day I was about to get spoiled and had begun to get a little finicky about my eatin' because there was so much good food and so many cooks fixin' it that I thought I just as well graze on what was best and leave the other alone. However, the fill that I was takin' wasn't helping those sick cattle much and I hadn't really come across anything that I had reason to believe was too poisonous.

With my primitive way of thinking and my knowledge and love of horses and cattle, I was spending more loafin' time around the corral talking to the Indian cowboys and playing with the little Indian kids than I was up there in that flyboy's palace. An Indian boy about seven years old and not very big for his age took me by the finger and led me around behind the ranch help's houses, where there was a nice flock of goats that the Indian help had and the little children herded up in the mountains during the day and brought in at night.

A fat young nanny goat was sprawled out in the corner of the corral throwing a wild kind of spasmodic fit. There were a few old squaws and small children watching her, but their expressions showed no signs of emotion. This little Indian boy was pretty sharp and spoke fair English. He told me that these goats had been dying this way about the same time as the steers had been dying, and sometimes it was one of their milk goats and some of the milk tasted wild. I didn't tell him but I thought I had found me an Indian medicine man of about seven years old.

One of the Indian ranch hands rode up horseback and I asked him if I could cut this goat open. He said, sure, that they were going to eat it anyway. He went ahead and butchered the goat and I examined the intestines and organs while he finished cutting up the goat, then the squaws took it to their little rock houses.

I didn't find anything wrong with that goat and common sense told me that couldn't be so because I had watched it have a fit and die. I went back to the palace and ate a big supper without mentioning this batch of experience.

The next morning when we rode into the cattle that were being pastured in close to the headquarters, I saw a steer that seemed a little wobbly and I rushed him horseback. When he ran about fifty feet, he stumbled and fell on the ground and went through the same kind of fit as the goat had. I cut him open, too, and examined the internal organs but found nothing wrong.

I went into town that day and bought up a batch of candy and trinkets for my little Indian friends. Late that afternoon as I saw the children bringing in the goats from the mountains, I walked down to the corral. There were three small boys and a girl with the little flock of goats. They all smiled and spoke to me and I went to passin' out some stick candy and jawbreakers that I had in my pocket.

The jawbreakers were of all colors of the rainbow and the girl, who might have been a year or two older than my little medicine man, took a yellowish-orange one and said it was about the color of the roots that the goats that had the fits ate. The boys all had a laugh, saying that maybe a candy that color would give her fits too. Small Indian children have a keen sense of humor, and when they are not afraid of you, they are lots of fun to be around.

I knew that the little Indians knew the plant that was making the goats have fits and the next morning I was down at the corral early when they turned the goats out to herd them up into the mountains. I knew that those little

Indian kids could outwalk and outclimb me in the rocks so I saddled a good gentle horse and rode along behind the goats and talked to my little medicine man.

When we were high up in the rocks, I reached in my pocket and passed out some more candy and held one of these yellowish-orange-colored jawbreakers and asked them to show me the weed that color. They weren't more than a minute pulling some wild potato vines out of the crevices between the rocks, and the root was a little round-shaped ball about the color of the candy.

The kids helped me gather about half a gallon of these roots, and I kept enough of the vines to stick in my pockets and poured the roots in a saddle pocket and started back to the headquarters.

My fat flyboy friend would not be in until later in the afternoon and I decided that it was time for me to get to my laboratory with these plants. I took a little more time going home and got there late the second day.

In my laboratory I started grinding and working what I had brought back with me. I had been gone six days and I had a stack of calls that I had to make. It took all of that night and most of the next day to catch up with my practice and then I came back to my Arizona plants.

Old flyboy flew in the next morning and I was able to report to him that it was the wild potato vines that were causing the trouble. The toxic substance worked on the central nervous system and the lack of coordination was coming from damage of the nervous system. The only treatment would be to move the stock away from the high rocky region where the melted snow had made the potato crop.

He was a little astonished but was convinced that I had found the trouble and began to plan how he could get his cattle away from that part of the range. He whipped out his checkbook and paid me for my services and asked, "Are there any favors that I can do for you?"

I said, "Yeah, one. When you get back to the ranch, let the Indian children herd their goats along the draws and round the spring where the milk will be good and the goats won't die from eating the potato vines. You see, it was your own medicine man and the goats that found the trouble for me."

Everett Townsend of Townsend Brothers, who operated several ranches up and down the border and owned a Ford agency in Mexico City, tended to lots of their business by plane. Everett flew into Fort Stockton to get me to fly down beyond Del Rio to look at a bunch of sheep that weren't dying but were very unthrifty.

He came in the office and we visited a little while and he told me about his sheep and said we could look at them and be back by noon. I told him I was much obliged for all that fast service, but I hadn't got my business scattered to where I had to tend to it in an airship and his loss and lack of time were no responsibility of mine. Besides, I had my word out to my propeller friends that I would always be on the ground to gather them up. I said that if he felt that these sheep would last till morning, I would drive down in my car and take a look at them.

Well, he gave me another one of those friendly lectures like the kind I'd been gettin' from the rest of the propeller boys around town, but it soaked in about the same way theirs had and I didn't have a change of heart about them propellers. I told him I would be at the ranch about middle of the morning next day, and he got somebody else to rush him back out to the airfield so he could hurry to tend to something else.

I left the office long before daylight and tended to two

horse calls on the way that didn't take up a whole lot of time and was at the ranch at Del Rio a little before noon. Everett lived in town and I called him there, but he hadn't been in since yesterday. The foreman at the ranch said he knew about the sheep but didn't know about Mr. Everett, so he and I went to see about the sheep.

They had been pastured on spear grass and had a good deal more than enough spear grass needles caught in their wool that were gradually working the points into the hide and flesh of these fat yearling muttons. This wasn't hard to find out walking around on the ground, which was a lot closer than cloud range for examining sheep.

I went back into Del Rio and by middle of the afternoon found out that Everett had gone by San Angelo when he left Fort Stockton and somewhere among the hops and jumps and landin' and risin', he had knocked a wheel off his airplane and was grounded somewhere unhurt but scratching his head and chewing his fingernails because of all the time he was losing not being able to tell somebody else to do something.

The foreman had already moved the sheep out of the spear-grass pasture, and I was back home on the ground tending to the rest of my practice when Everett called me a few days later. We discussed what had been done and he said, "Send me a bill."

I said, "You don't mind if I don't send it airmail, do you?"

One morning about daylight, I walked in on the coffee crowd and could tell by the look on their faces that something pretty serious was before the meeting. Two or three who were facing me waved to me to come over and sit down. I said, "I ain't goin' to drink none of that damn coffee. That's for old men and women and nervous people. I'm goin' to eat some breakfast."

Someone spoke up and said, "You'd be nervous too if

you'd cleared land, drilled a well, and bought tractors and stuff to plant sorghum to kill sheep instead of fatten them."

Othro Adams was in the crowd, and since he had a plane and flew everywhere he went, his conversation was either about flying or sheep. Since I didn't think a man ought to be further off the ground than horseback, I thought I ought to include him in my morning's goin' over and said, "When people get their business mixed up with propellers and plows in a desert country, they ought not to expect anything to come out right. Anyhow, I can't see why you're so worried when you've got way the best horse doctor in the West with a damn good laboratory that would be available for a reasonable fee."

A good many ranchers had drilled irrigation wells and put land into cultivation on the pretense that they were going to raise their own feed because of the long distances that livestock feed stuffs had to be hauled in the Southwest and the ever-presence of drouth. Very few, if any of them, knew the real cost of equipping a farm or the overhead of operating one or they wouldn't have been so anxious to turn their attention from occasionally having to oil a windmill to the real job of pumping irrigation water with big equipment that required constant attention. However, the fad was on to bulldoze good mesquite land and turn it bottom-side upward to raise feed.

I didn't understand all there was to know about the government farm program and cared a good deal less, but this land was not eligible to be planted to some of the other feed crops and grain sorghum crops were planted on most of these new "pump" farms. The land was fresh and fertile and the sunshine was ever-persistent, and with irrigation water bountiful, crops of grain sorghum soon dotted the otherwise range landscapes.

These crops came on in the summer after my yellowweed

research activities had become dormant. When these crops had enough growth to be putting out heads of grain, ranchers began turning their flocks of sheep in for grazing because the principal purpose of the crops was to make summer grazing or to be baled for hay.

After the sheep had been on this lush feed a few days, there would be an occasional dead one with no apparent outward cause for death; the rest of the sheep grazing in the same field would seem to be in good condition.

Throughout the years I had been in the Trans-Pecos Region I had been forced to do extensive research on most of the livestock troubles because the available sources of veterinary knowledge had never touched the semi-arid region of the Far Southwest. It had gotten to be a common statement among ranchers, "Have Doc run it through his lab and find out what it's got in it," and so it was natural for me to be called to start analyzing these sorghum fields.

I did post-mortems on these sheep and found no slight indications of poisoning or gastrointestinal upsets. About all I could say was that they were dead, and this wasn't a soothing remark.

I analyzed the tender blades of the sorghum growth, the stalks, and even the sparse heads of grain and for weeks had not found out any more than I knew in the beginning. The sheep that were dying didn't constitute a die-out and didn't reach epidemic proportions, but a few just continued to die on these fresh fields, and limiting the grazing to a few hours a day didn't help, nor did anything else that we tried in the way of management practices.

I saved a good many sheep that we got to after they became sick, but I didn't explain to my rancher friends that I was using what would be termed "shotgun" medical treatment, treatment that would have cured any one of twenty things and was nonspecific for any particular condition.

After many tests, I still hadn't learned the toxic content of these irrigated grain sorphum crops. I drove out early and late to watch the sheep and study their habits until some of my friends began to be afraid that maybe I was eatin' that sorghum too.

Most everybody was willing to cooperate and take their sheep off the fields or turn them back on when I asked them to, and this should have helped a lot; only I still hadn't learned much. Several ranchers were loafing in my office one afternoon when the subject of the death loss of these sheep came up.

I chimed up and said, "Believe I've found out all there is to know about the grazin' of grain sorghum. If you'll let me know when you want to turn in your sheep, I'll run a test and see if your fields are ready."

One of them said, "I'm sure glad that you've smartened up. I was beginnin' to think that it was goin' to take another year's lamb crop for us to educate you."

"Well," I said, "I didn't use to be so slow until I went to associatin' with sheepherders-turned-farmers, but you haven't ruined me entirely or I wouldn't know what to do about the grain sorghum."

By late summer we were following this practice without any death loss, and the ranchers were shipping fat sheep off of irrigated grain sorghum fields and braggin' on old Doc and his lab for being able to cope with their troubles. Of course, I didn't discourage this kind of conversation too much and by the following year nobody dared turn sheep into a grain sorghum field without first having me test it.

This went on for a number of years before I left the Trans-Pecos Region and nobody knew that the birds of the air were doing my testing for me. By close observation I had found that when wild birds would light on the heads and peck the grain, the toxic substances, whatever they were, would be gone out of the plant and it was sufficiently matured to be grazed. The only testing I was doing was driving out to see if the sorghum was fit for the birds to eat.

I got a call about midnight from a druggist friend of mine in El Paso and from the noise in the background, I could very well picture that there was a whole lot of people having a more than common amount of fun.

During the party they had gotten to talking about horses. One of the socialite women in the party told about her saddle mare developing a very serious eye condition and said that during the last few weeks she had had several vets examine the mare's eye. It seemed to the druggist from the conversation that this was truly a fine jet black American saddle mare and the social doll was not joking about trying to get something done for her mare.

Well, this druggist friend of mine spoke up and told her that he knew the best horse doctor in the world and if there was any way on earth to save that mare's eye, she needed to see me quick. This champagne conversation had gotten so serious that they were calling me at midnight to talk to me about the mare's eye. He began with a few opening remarks and then told me there was a lady who wanted to talk to me, and about that time a lot of personality began to purr and erupt over the phone. (I don't think that the champagne had much effect on her because she was still like that several days later.)

For about thirty minutes she told me how much she loved this mare and then for another ten minutes she explained who all had looked at the horse's eye. She said the general opinion was that there was a tumor in the socket behind the eyeball. After I was thoroughly informed as to all the treatments the mare had endured, she gushed forth that she would have her plane pick me up in the morning so I could some see the mare's eye.

I said, "I don't believe you will. There never has been a plane able to pick me up."

This was when she showed some fog from the champagne: she couldn't quite fathom what I meant, so she gave me back to my druggist friend. I told him I could get up to see the mare in a few days, but I wasn't going to come by plane. He thought it was kind of funny and said he would explain it to her and hung up. I thought this was just a bunch of long-distance champagne conversation and went back to sleep and forgot it.

The second morning after this conversation, a beautiful thing that didn't want to quit being young floated in my office, and from the purr in her voice, I recognized her as being the same one who I had spoken to on the phone. She began telling me that she felt that I would surely ride in the plane with her, and I said, "Hon, there may be some things that you and I could do together, but it ain't goin' to be flyin'."

This didn't set her down too much and I think she had begun to wonder how much charm it was going to take to get me to look at that mare's eyeball. Since she had taken a taxi to town, and I was goin' to be driving, I thought it would be safe for me to take her back to the airport. On the way out we made arrangements for me to go up to El Paso as soon as possible to work on the mare's eye.

The following Saturday afternoon, I called her from the Del Norte Hotel and told her I was in town, and she gave me directions to the stable where she kept her horse. The stable attendant led out this beautiful black American saddle mare that had been under blanket with all the care and attention that a fine horse could be given, and, sure enough, she had a badly swelled eye that was running a stream of tear-gland solution.

I examined the eye carefully and used light and a magnifying glass. Even though this mare was experiencing a great deal of pain from that bad eye, her manners and training were such that she was as patient and obedient as she could possibly be while I worked around her eye.

The examination did not convince me that there was a tumor growth in the socket and I could not detect any signs of infection that should have been present when so much irritation was apparent. The druggist friend once saw me remove a tumor from an eye socket and save the horse's eye, and this was why he had thought of me the night of the champagne party.

I explained to the Prima Donna that it would be necessary to put the mare under anesthesia for me to go in behind the eye into the eye socket. I had no encouragement to offer and no promises to make, but if she wanted the operation performed, I would do whatever I could to save the eye. She told me she would prefer not to watch but would like to know what was in that mare's head besides her eyeball and for me to do whatever I deemed necessary.

By now the druggist and a whole carload of the socialite crowd had gotten out to get their eyes used to the sunlight and were standing around in front of the stable visiting.

The stable operator and his attendants were all very helpful. We swept off a large section of plank floor in the hall of the barn and bedded it with loose hay and then put out horse blankets on top of the hay to keep it from stirring up and being in the way.

We led this gentle mare out into the middle of the blankets without her offering any resistance or showing any bad manners, and I very carefully gave her an injection of chloral hydrate. As she began to lay down, we maneuvered her around in order to get her down with her bad eye on the up-side. Rarely did I ever get a chance to do large-animal surgery under sanitary conditions, so I just took all precautions that I could and hoped for the best.

I had my instruments in a good antiseptic solution that would not burn the tissue of the eye socket and I rolled the upper eyelid back and was very careful in examining the socket above and behind the eye for a possible fibrous fleshy growth.

As I determined that I had found the trouble, I began to probe with some smooth round forceps that would not damage any tissue. When I got these forceps firmly fixed on the object with one hand and held the eyelid back with the other, I decided to see if this object was movable, hoping to dislodge it without too much surgery.

As I worked it forward, I used a very light touch and allowed whatever cartilage that might be caught in the forceps to slip out as gently as possible from around the object, and then very easily lifted it out. I hurriedly dropped it in my bucket of solution and began to clean the eye with medicated agents. Even though this mare was asleep, her breathing eased and I could see the muscles of her neck relax.

I had not intended for the anesthesia to last very long, so the barn attendants began to roll her over back and forth by her feet and legs and massage her, and I gave her some stimulant. The champagne crowd at the door of the barn had for the most part lost their voices, and other than an occasional gurgle of some strong liquid, they were silent.

In a few minutes the mare came up on her feet, and though she was groggy, she was standing very relaxed. I wiped the small amount of blood off her face that had been caused by the probing, and after she had her complete balance, we walked her up and down the hall of the barn a few times and then put her back in a dark stall.

I picked up my bucket of antiseptic solution and thought I would turn the stomach of some of that socialite crowd by walking out in the sunlight and pull out whatever it was that I got out of that mare's eye in front of Prima Donna and her friends. I felt around in this milky-like solution and to my surprise came up with a pretty blue and white glass marble—the kind that kids play in the sand with.

I turned to this astonished bunch of champagners and said in a very unconcerned voice, "It happens all the time where horses are allowed to play marbles."

Nobody knew then and nobody has found out since how the marble got behind that mare's eyeball.

Thousands of sheep had been shipped from the desert up into the irrigated plains of the Panhandle of Texas and in 'most any hotel lobby around Lubbock or Plainview or any of the rest of the High Plains all the way to Kansas, you could go in and find someone you knew from the desert Southwest.

A bunch of these transplanted visitors were in the Plainview irrigated area grazing lambs and other sheep on irrigated winter wheatfields. They called me one night after suppertime. There were three or four of them up there talkin' to me on the phone about their troubles—not askin' me too much about what to do about them—but just tellin' me that I had to do somethin'.

John Gahr was having the worst fit among 'em because he had lots of sick sheep, and I believe sick sheep gave John Gahr the bellyache, the heartburn, and runnin' fits worse than anybody I ever knew. Each one of them made these sheep sound a little worse, and by the time John Gahr got to the phone, I didn't think they would have any left if I started up right then.

One of the other boys came back on the phone and said they'd have a plane down for me early in the morning. Plainview wasn't more than three hundred miles from Fort Stockton and I told him I guessed he could send a plane to take the drench back that I would use after I got there. I said that I didn't suppose that a high elevation would curdle it too much but it sure would curdle my stomach to come in an airship, so I would be there when I could get there in a car.

He said, "I don't believe you know how sick these sheep are."

Then John Gahr came back on to tell me about how sick the sheep were, and I said, "I can tell from here that they aren't as sick as you bunch of desert rats that's got your money tied up in them."

This caused a little laughin' and carryin' on and they admitted that might be part of the trouble, and I promised them I would get there as soon as I could make the trip in my car.

Next afternoon we all met at the hotel and had a round of refreshments and a main course of conversation about the sheep. They told me the sheep were standing on their toes with their bellies drawed in and their backs humped up, and some of them showed the effects of a little fever on their noses and mouths.

These lambs and yearlings had been born in the Trans-Pecos Region in a drouth and some of their mothers had been born in the same drouth before them. During their days as suckling lambs, they had gotten little milk and hardly any tender weeds or grass. They were undersized when they were shipped to the Plains Region to go on irrigated lush winter wheatfields.

We drove around to the fields to see several different flocks and the situation was pretty nearly the same in about twenty thousand sheep. There were as many as 20 per cent in any and all the flocks that were in this stiff, sore condition.

Back at the hotel I explained to the boys that these sheep had taken in so little of the proper mineral content in their early diet to build bone, cartilage, and tissue that they didn't have enough room in their intestinal tract for all the green wheat that they were standing on, and they didn't have enough frame to put on flesh as fast as this lush wheat would furnish it to them. They had spent all their lives gettin' this way and I just wanted to point out to them how little good it would have done for me to have saved six hours by flying up there.

They all slobbered and said, "All right, all right. You've made your point and we didn't send after you to listen to you lecture us about our man-made mistakes. We've done put the word out that you're a genius, so you got no way out but to make these sheep start doing good."

I got on the phone and called a laboratory in Kansas City to send me a one hundred thousand cc. of ovine natural serum. Then I called the Tennessee Valley Authority at Knoxville, Tennessee, and asked them to send us a shipment of the very purest dicalcium phosphate that they had mined. I got in touch with other sources of supply for vitamins and other digestive aids and asked that they be shipped the fastest possible way and told my air-minded friends that it was too bad it would be too heavy to come by plane.

I had about a fourth of the needed normal serum the

next morning and I'm afraid it came by airmail, so I didn't bring up the subject around the breakfast table at the hotel. My purpose in shooting these sheep with normal serum was to furnish them enough animal fluid to incorporate with the available protein already saturated in the tissues, which was causing the stiffness. This would put the sheep back to grazing as fast as they were treated.

Within five days we had a mineral amino-acid vitamin-supplement mixture put out in containers in the fields near the watering places and the ready intake of this preparation put the sheep back to gaining weight on the wheatfields to which the sheepmen had bought the grazing rights at premium prices.

Since I had proved again that I was the genius they had claimed I was and had also settled their nerves and improved their digestion, I told them I would include it on the bill at a later date and drove back to the tranquil existence of the desert and drouth.

CORN, COB,
SHUCK AND ALL

In the early spring a few plants were attempting to grow and there was some sparse green stuff in the draws and around the edges of the irrigation ditches in the fields. The Leon Farms a few miles west of Fort Stockton were watered by the Leoncita Springs. A large earthen dam that had been constructed many years before impounded the spring water that was used for irrigation on the Leon Farms long before irrigation wells were drilled for supplementary water. It had been a dry, warm winter and spring vegetation was coming up a month or so earlier than usual.

The Leon Farms were nonresident-owned and managed exclusively by Mr. Beeman. He was a very efficient business administrator and farmer and didn't make any pretense of being a cowman or stockman, and he was very willing to discuss details and receive advice and help with his livestock problems. Mr. Beeman drove up to my office in the late morning hours and told me that he had over a hundred cattle in the pasture surrounding Leon Lake and several of them were showing signs of sickness. He asked me if I would come and look at the cattle and see what could be done for them.

As we walked along the ditches that were used for irrigation beneath the lake dam, there was but little green vegetation and I saw no evidence that the cattle were eating on any brush that would be considered poisonous. However, there was a good supply of desirable browse plants in this part of the pasture. We had already "posted" a dead cow and found extreme swelling in the liver and a highly inflamed intestinal tract with thickened walls.

The cattle were reasonably gentle and we walked around through them without any difficulty. Many of them were breathing extremely hard and I could tell by observation that they had a high heart ratio and were nervous.

Any lake dam will seep a little water to the lower side,

and as we got into this part of the pasture, there was a lush crop of tender young yellowish-green cocklebur plants growing in profusion on several acres below and up on the dam. I told Mr. Beeman that this was his trouble and that the cattle ought to be treated after they had been moved out of this pasture and given a few days' rest on good feed.

He immediately instructed his helpers to slowly drive these cattle along the irrigation ditch and across the road to another pasture. While they were doing this, he told me that there was nothing in that pasture for them to eat but he did have plenty of alfalfa in the barns which he would put them on. He asked me whether medication would be necessary if they began to straighten up on dry feed.

I explained to him that taking them off the poison weed and putting them on alfalfa would stop any further accumulation of toxic effects but that the animal body would not eliminate the poison already consumed without medical attention. Mr. Beeman readily understood this and told me he would have men ready to help doctor these cattle when I deemed it best.

One cow died after they were moved and before we treated them, which was three days later. Mr. Beeman explained to me that this condition had never occurred before because there had always been an abundance of other vegetation, and it wouldn't happen again because he would fence off the land that was infested with the cockleburs and it would never be grazed again.

Since I had begun practicing at Fort Stockton, I had served very few unpleasant people. However, there were some that I could never do quite enough for, and when I kept their livestock from dying, they usually were quick to tell me that they thought they would have gotten well anyway but maybe I helped them some. The veterinary profession is a hard one in that many times owners do not appreciate what is done and livestock can neither tell what is the matter with them, what mankind has fed them, nor thank you for the relief they experience.

I had one client in particular—general manager for a large farming and ranching operation—who considered himself just a little more intelligent than anybody that he was discussing his troubles with, but he was very charitable in that he allowed you to converse with him. However, from my point of view he lacked a damn sight being as smart as he thought.

When I answered a call to his place, he would call in his stock foreman and another helper or two and he was always in attendance himself. As I treated whatever type of domestic animal that was sick, he very carefully cross-examined me with direct questions as to the disease, cause, diagnosis, and treatment. He was very careful to get the exact dosage and the proper name of all medical agents I used.

There was a huge ledger on a desk in the farm office where immediately after my departure he went and wrote up the entire case; "Information" was the title of that ledger. In his estimation, this made it unnecessary to ever call on a professional individual to treat that type of case again, since he and his foreman would refer back to "Information" and get the diagnosis and what drugs to administer.

One day he called me on the phone and told me that he had a cow with milk fever (his diagnosis) and I should come out and bring an intravenous apparatus with a 16-gauge two-inch hypodermic needle and 350-cc. of calcium gluconate. I had once treated a cow for him that had milk fever and knew the reason he called me was because he was caught short by not having already purchased an intra-venous outfit.

The mail hack was leaving in a few minutes from the Post Office and would go by the farm, so I just wrapped up everything that he asked for, put it on the mail hack, and sent it to him and he had it as soon as I could have an-swered the call. He came in in a few days and in a very guarded conversation did admit that there might have been a slight possibility that they had misdiagnosed the cow's case since it was a fact that she died.

I was trying to get loose from this particular operator and had already made arrangements to do without his practice and thought that this little episode might break him of the habit of calling me. However, in about three weeks I got another call from him and he had evidently overcome whatever ill feelings he had toward me from that last incident.

When I drove into the headquarters, he was at the barn with his helpers and waved at me to come on down there. As usual, he was well dressed in a business suit with a white shirt and a bow tie, was clean shaven and even smelled good. He had a coming two-year-old heifer in labor with her first calf and it was easy to see that the farm and ranch hands had done everything in their power to deliver this calf. I could tell at a glance that the calf had been dead several days and that calling me was the last resort to try to save the heifer.

I explained to Mr. Information that it would be a useless effort on my part because gangrene had set in and there was no way of saving the heifer. He was very respectful of my opinion and granted me that this was probably a total loss except for the fact that much information could be gained by a Caesarean operation that would be useful in the future management and calving of young cattle and he was very insistent that I do a Caesarean section.

After administering sufficient anesthesia by intravenous injection, I shaved the heifer's side and belly and very professionally and expertly started the operation.

Mr. Information securely stood a good distance away on the offwind side and held a spotless white handkerchief over his nose and mouth to protect his sensitive system from the unpleasant odors. He would step up to my back and pull on the sleeve that I had rolled up past my elbows to get my attention as he asked me questions. I was very deliberate and technical in my explanations and answered every question that he asked me very explicitly.

When this useless operation was completed and I had sutured the incision just as though the cow were going to live a normal lifetime, I went over to the water pump to clean off the rough part of the aftermath of the surgical performance. He came over and complimented me very eloquently for my professional knowledge and ability and said to send him a bill. With this he bid me adieu and went back to the more comfortable and pleasant atmosphere of his office.

I went into town and that night wrote out and mailed him a bill—fifty dollars for the Caesarean operation, one hundred dollars for the lecture. I got my check in the return mail and was forever free of Mr. Information and his practice.

Just after sundown I was sittin' out in front of the office enjoyin' the breeze that always comes up from the desert at this time of day when Chiquita, a sweet little Mexican girl about five years old, came up to my chair waggin' her kitty cat, and in her English-Spanish mixed baby jabber put her fingers around on some sores on her cat's head that she wanted doctored.

I could tell at a glance that these were ringworms, and unbeknownst to most people, cats have been supplying babies with ringworms since time began, so I was laughin' and teasin' Chiquita and ran my hand under her hairline above her forehead and there was a little sore on her too. I had some ringworm medicine; it was almost a clear light liquid but would make a little bit of an amber stain on the skin.

I painted the ringworms on the cat. Then painted Chiquita's ringworms and told her that the sores on the cat would get well faster if we treated hers too. She thought that was funny and rolled her big brown eyes and smiled and showed me another one behind her ear. She thought this was great fun and the medicine didn't burn but very little and she turned and ran back up the street carrying her cat about half a block to where her momma and daddy ran a little Mexican eating place and bar.

The next morning at sunup as I came out of the office door, Chiquita was coming up waggin' her little bitty baby brother and said that he had kitty sores too. He was a little baby with one ringworm right on his fat cheek. I thought this was going to be fun so I dropped a little green dye into the ringworm medicine and told Chiquita that I would doctor Little Chappo with pretty medicine. She thought this was funny and said that it was pretty and she wanted some "pretty" on her, too; so I treated her ringworms with the green medicine. The cat had followed her and I gave it another treatment also.

In a few days Chiquita's mother was passing the office door, stopped and stuck her head in and said, "Dok-tor, I want to thank you 'too much' and next time I have baby I think we call you."

I was answering from one to three calls a day to Burdine's Dairy, and even though they were short calls, it was too many to one dairy to treat cows that were having a variety of internal upsets, including lots of bloat. Old man Burdine kept tellin' me that he had not changed the feed; he was feeding them alfalfa hay between milking times and he was feeding ground ear corn, which was ground corn cob, shuck and all, with cottonseed meal and other additives. He had been feeding this same feed for a year, and in his argumentative way, he knew it couldn't be the feed.

The cattle were not on pasture and were standing in a dry lot eating baled alfalfa hay between milkings, so the trouble had to be caused by the feed. I started through his feed barn and mixing operation and everything was just as he had said it was, and for the want of something smarter to do, I took samples of the separate feed materials and took them to my laboratory after this condition had been prevalent for over a week.

This corn, cob, shuck, and all, that was coarsely ground began to worry me, so I decided to run a few chemical tests. I didn't find any prussic, picric, or any of the other common acids that would usually cause trouble. An old cowboy alcoholic with a sensitive nose came in the front door of my office, and as he came through the middle door to the laboratory, he said, "Doc, I smell some kind of a cheap grade of drinkin' whisky. Have you got on that stuff?"

I said, "Hell no, it's just your breath blowin' back in your face."

He said, "It ain't either. You're about to turn to a private drinker hidin' back here in this dive where you won't have to divide with nobody."

I said, "Well, I ain't gonna divide with you. You've already made fun of the quality of my whisky and you haven't even seen it."

He picked up a handful of that ground corn off the end of the lab table and stuck it up to his nose and said, "You're worse'n a bootlegger. You're puttin' it in cow feed."

This was the very lead I needed, but I wasn't about to let him know it, so I said, "If it would steady your nerves any, we'll go up to the Stockton Pharmacy and I'll buy you some fresh brewed coffee that hasn't been made in a tin bucket and it'll have a different taste than what you've been used to."

We walked from the Medical Arts up to the drugstore and I socialized with him just long enough to be pleasant, then broke back to run some different tests on that ground corn. I had to go back out to the dairy to get a fresh supply of corn and after about three hours of laboratory work and half a bushel of ground corn, I came up with a vial of stuff that I identified as acetone, which is a few molecule chemical structures from being alcohol.

Late that afternoon about milking time, I went out and told old man Burdine that his trouble was in his ground corn. He sputtered and slobbered and said that it couldn't be that because this was a fresh batch of corn he got about ten days ago from the feed mill. I asked him right quick what day it was he called me for a first case of bloat. He studied a minute and said, "I'll be damn. It was about ten days ago."

I asked him if there was any way he could manage to feed that night without using any more corn. He said, "Yeah, I'll just give 'em the same amount of other feed and more alfalfa hay and they won't miss the corn much."

He added, however, that the bulkiness of the ground

corn, cob, shuck, and all made it a lot easier to mix the other feed.

I was out early the next morning and there were no cases of bloat. As we talked, he said he still had to have some more corn and if what he had was causing the poison, he would try to get it from some other source. He had lost quite a bit of milk production in ten days and two cows had died.

I told him I wasn't practicin' law, but I thought he had reason for the feed mill to pay him some damages. Besides that, the feed mill might be selling this same corn to other feeders and we had better take it up with them. He said, "Yeah, you go on in and tell 'em what you found, so they won't think I'm crazy like they will when I go to tryin' to tell 'em, and I'll come in after I get through milking."

I went to the feed mill and was careful to present the case to the feed-mill manager, who listened with interest and showed no signs of trying to deny that the corn might be the trouble. However, he told me that he was buying this corn by the carload in hundred-pound sacks already ground and it was being shipped to him by a feed brokerage company in Lubbock. He wasn't sure who the brokerage company was selling it for, but, as best he could remember, the last car had an Iowa billing on it.

I happened to know the feed brokerage company since I had done business with them and told him that with his permission I would talk to them on the phone. He said, "Yeah, go ahead. We need to trace this corn down and put the blame and cost of damages on the proper parties."

I thought it would be best to tend to this over my own phone, so I went back to the office. In talking with the brokerage firm manager, he said that they had not loaded, unloaded, ground, or in any manner handled these corn consignments and it was being shipped by a mill in Iowa to them.

I went back to the feed mill and old man Burdine had come in from milking and we all discussed his trouble. I told them that it would not be wise to make a phone call to the Iowa mill because if they had any more of that particular corn they could dispose of it and hedge against any liability concerning the loss of milk and the two cows.

Old man Burdine said, "Doc, it'd be good to have you out of town a few days, and maybe you haven't seen Iowa, so why don't you go up there, and if you stay out of the country long enough maybe my cows will straighten out and be all right."

I said right quick that his talk didn't fool me none. He wasn't as interested in my seein' Iowa as he was in seein' his cows straighten'n' out and start back to giving milk.

I drove into Iowa after midday the next afternoon. I found the feed mill and went in the office and introduced myself and met the man who owned the mill. He was a nice fellow and an old-time mill operator and I explained my mission to him.

He said, "Well, if I'd known there was such a man, I'd have already sent for you. We've got a lot of steers in feed lots around close that are havin' all kinds of trouble and there have been several steers die and nobody's put their hand on the cause."

He called his mill foreman in and talked about the corn that they were grinding. It developed that this corn had been stored in an old warehouse and lots of water had dripped in and been blown in from snow through the winter and spring, but since they had corn stored in outside wire granaries and even in small silos made out of red panel fence, they hadn't felt that the water damages could have been of any consequence to this corn. If it was true, this would be the first time that they had ever experienced any trouble from grinding corn that had been damp from weather.

I was fast to explain the difference in their storaging process and pointed out that the water seeping through the ear corn under a shed and surrounded by solid walls would be more likely to go through a fermentation process than corn stored in the open, where the wind and sun could hit it. This all made sense, and without much argument, the mill owner was glad for me to have samples of freshly ground corn that was going through the mill at this particular moment. It was easy to see that he had quite a bit more at stake than the losses at one dairy in Texas.

I took the corn samples and drove into Omaho, where I knew a lab technician from years past, and we extracted the same faint-smellin' stuff that Old Alcoholic had sniffed in my office. The mill owner was quick to call the feeders that had this corn in their feed lots and instruct his mill foreman to start grinding corn that he had stored in other buildings and told me that an immediate settlement would be made with my client in Texas. This old gentleman was a businessman and fair in his dealings.

I thought I was far enough from home, and as old Burdine wanted me to be gone an extra day or so, I went by Kansas City and then worked my way back to Fort Stockton about the third day. It was right after noon and I went to the feed mill to give a report and the old Iowa corn miller was sittin' in the office with old Burdine.

They were discussing what the damages would amount to and old Burdine was trying to be as fair as Mr. Iowa. They asked me what my fees were in the case and I told them and Mr. Iowa said, "I'll include it in Mr. Burdine's check."

In a few days I got a nice letter of appreciation with a

one hundred dollar check in it from the Iowa corn miller. This was the most pleasant mishap in my entire veterinary practice that I ever experienced with people where cattle, feed, milk, and money were concerned.

The seasons of the year had ceased to have much meaning because they were all dry. We talked about the possibility of rain at equinox. The seasons of the year were passed as designated by the calendar, but in truth the drouth and the desert had given the year only two seasons, winter and summer, both dry. What few livestock that were in the country after winter set in could be generally assumed that the ranchers and their bankers had decided to stay with another year and my winter practice was a matter of survival on accidental cases of injury to livestock and other emergency-type calls.

The economic influence of ten years of drouth had more than separated the men from the boys, and the common run of jokes about dry weather only produced a grin instead of a laugh in a crowd. Occasionally somebody would buy a new pickup or a new car, and when it came up in conversation, people would ask in not quite a half-joking manner, "Where did ya get the money?"

The best answer was, "I've been savin' my feed sacks since the drouth started and I just sold them all," and there had been enough feed sacks bought on some ranches to have paid for a new car or truck.

Most of the concentrated feed being put out for range livestock was ground maize, cottonseed meal, and salt. The salt content would run about 25 per cent and in some cases was stepped up to 33⅓ per cent. The reason for this huge amount of salt was because feed was being put out in self-feeders. Since the pastures were so big and the livestock population was so small, a rancher couldn't very well drive to them and hunt up what needed to be fed and these self-feeders were usually placed in reasonable distance from the water troughs.

Some form of hay or ground bundles of feed were being used as roughage, but true to their nature sheep and cattle constantly walked the range and tore up the ground with their sharp hooves hunting a bite of something green. Whenever I posted a cow or a sheep, there was always an unusual amount of indigestible sticks that were small enough to be bitten off a bush, and sometimes an entire impaction would be black brush or mesquite bark that had been gnawed from the lower limbs of the trees. Medicines and medical science were of little benefit in these sorts of cases.

When the spring winds started and the earth that had been mulched by trampling hooves on the trails to and from the water troughs and feed grounds began to blow, I began to get another kind of practice. I was called out to Burnt House Draw, about thirty miles west of Fort Stockton near the railroad switch of Hoovey, to see some poor-grade Mexican steers that were dying.

It was generally thought among cowmen that these native Mexican cattle could live longer and do better under bad range conditions than any other class of livestock, but when they started dying, it about wiped out any doubt in the rancher's mind about having enough feed on the range to keep a few livestock.

These Mexican cattle were about three years old and maybe weighed six hundred pounds, and their appearance gave a very pronounced impression of heads, horns, pot bellies with little frame and no flesh. In fact, there wasn't a whole lot of difference in the appearance of a live one and a dead one. I got down on my knees in the dirt and went to cutting open a Mexican steer, more for the want of something to do than any idea that I would discover any different causes for these cattle dying.

The Mexican steer was still holding his reputation for being able to digest anything that he could chew because there was no impaction in this steer, but as a matter of routine examination, I dissected his lungs and laid them out on top of the carcass. I made a cross-section cut and took one lobe of the lung about half in two. I reached over and put my hand on the lung to shift a little weight from standing on my knees while I did the post-mortem, and the pressure of my hand caused thin mud to secrete from the tissues of the lung. Then as I began to make further study of the lung, I even found deposits of solid earth in some of the tissue. In most cases these deposits would be surrounded by pus, and the supposedly toughest of all breeds of livestock were dying from dust pneumonia.

As long as the late-winter and early-spring winds blew and sheep and cattle followed one another in the dust-filled trails back and forth across the range, we continued to lose livestock. Sheep died much worse than cattle, perhaps because of their lack of resistance, but principally because their heads were closer to the ground, where the density of the dust was the greatest from the stock that were traveling in front of them stirring it up.

Cactus had come into its own as a range feed and thousands of acres of it had been fed by burning the stickers off with butane flame-throwers that were by now in common everyday use. After sheep and cattle learned to enjoy the juicy leaves of pear cactus, sometimes they wouldn't wait for mankind to burn off the stickers and "pear mouths" became another malady in the stock business.

The mouths and throats of livestock would become lined with broken-off stickers and this could counteract any good effects to be had from the juices and the food value of the cactus. However, driving hunger seemed to reduce the pain and pear-mouthed cattle and sheep seemed to ignore the stickers in their effort to survive.

The seasons changed by the months on the calendar and the winds settled some, but the only greenery that was proof of spring was the pale, thin leaves that came out on what was left of the mesquite brush. This siege of drouth had developed more ulcers in people and untimely deaths from heart conditions and the usual infirmities of age were hastened by the living conditions of drouth in a rugged breed of people. Most ranchers had begun to know that they and their families would show the effects of drouth even after the country was lush and with green feed in some future years to come.

Rainmakers made their appearance in the spring and there were various promotional ideas brought about in the theory of seeding clouds that would occasionally form and float around over the desert. Aviators moved into the country with rain-promotion experts and money was raised by various groups of ranchers. These aviators would fly into cloud formations and seed them with dry ice and a short cloud burst over a small area would be produced from this procedure.

Since there were not enough clouds to go around and not enough moisture in the sky, ranchers and farmers then began to take envious views of the way that this possible artificial rainfall was being distributed and bitter arguments arose among friends. The possibility that such procedures might be preventing enough cloud formations to really produce a beneficial rain for the country was even discussed. Cloud seeding finally amounted to nothing more than a man-made agitation to be borne by a rugged breed that nature had not been able to conquer.

THE DESERT

When a region is referred to as desert, with few exceptions it will arouse all the civic-minded people at the Chamber of Commerce, and all the one-man Chamber of Commerces in hearing distance will rear up to explain that the desert is some other region and this country that you have so rudely referred to as being desert is semi-arid. Now, "semi," hell! "Semi" would be the real good years in which enough rain falls and it would be on rare occasions that such reagions could be referred to as "semi."

The West has many stories and legends that are built on the lack of rain. When a newcomer first hears some of these old tales, his reaction is that they are sure stretchin' it. Then after he's been there a few years, he will come up with a story of his own that's worse than the ones the natives originated.

In a year when a desert region does get rain, vegetation will be lush. Weeds, cactus, and bushes will be ornamented with blooms of various hews of yellow and a few varieties will have white and pale-red blooms. Not all plants bearing a yellow bloom are toxic, but it can be safely stated that the majority of toxic plants do have yellow blooms the years that there is enough moisture for them to produce a bloom and thereafter seed.

The seeds of the desert plants and especially those of toxic desert plants will lay on the ground for a minimum of ten years or until time unknown, and the theory or thought that drouth could ever be long enough to kill the weed seedbed in a desert is folly of the human mind.

Before the desert was stocked with the human race, much of these remote regions were never grazed by many of the wild species of animal life. The grazing animals of the desert were principally deer and antelope and the lowly burro.

Deer and antelope could do without water for longer

periods of time and then travel great distances for an occasional fill. The digestive tract of the burro is so constructed that he thrives best on coarse forage of low food content and can smell water from one mountain range to another. It might be well to note that the buffalo or any other animal that requires huge amounts of forage never inhabited the Trans-Pecos and regions west of there.

The sheepherders that came to the desert following the years of rain thought they had found a shepherd's paradise. It was true that it was a good herder's country for a while since they were uninhibited by fences, definite ownerships, and landmarks and could follow the rains and reduce the heat of the summer by drifting into the higher mountainous regions and then cheat the winters by herding back into the desert's sunbathed flats.

This form of range operation did not last for a long period since mankind is probably the most destructive of all the animal species. He began to build fences and confine flocks and herds to tromp out the better grasses that were not too resistant to abuse, and capably made way for the less desirable and more worthless varieties of vegetation to take over as the good grazing plants disappeared.

This process has been described by the great thinkers as progress, and in a sense this might be right since it was progressively worse for the preservation of the natural and desirable vegetation of the Far Southwest. From my experience and observation I think that the deserts have been mined, so to speak, by the reckless misuse of earlier generations and because of the fact that the good grasses and other plants that have been destroyed will not re-cover the thin soils and rocky surfaces that it had taken nature millions of years to provide a sparse range for a few wild grazing species of animals.

The desert region affects all animal life that is forced to

survive in such areas. The walls of the hooves of horses become thicker and tougher to withstand the wear of pebbly rocks, hard ground, and the rimrock of the canyon regions as well as the rocky surfaces of the mountains. As this occurs through several generations of horses, the hoof becomes much smaller in width and the sole of the hoof becomes much more concave, which enables the walls to better protect the sole of the hoof, and the receded frog in the hoof is less susceptible to stone bruise and blisters.

After a few generations, the hoof on a horse of such regions is referred to by horsemen as a desert hoof, rock hoof, or sometimes a mountain hoof. The natives of the region consider it a compliment when a horse is referred to as mule-footed.

Deer are lightweight and fleet of foot with great maneuverability, which enables them to better protect their feet, but the cloven hoof of deer, antelope, or domestic cattle and sheep becomes tighter, so to speak, since the hoof does not spread from sand pressure between the toes. Many times points from on the inside of the cleft region of the toe are harder than they would be in terrain that was soft and where there was more moisture to enable the walls of the hoof to soften and spread.

The teeth of all animals, domestic or wild, through several generations of survival on desert forage become tighter set in the gums and closer together at the table of the tooth and will endure without as much as breaking when grazing on native desert plants than those from regions of lush grass and tender browse.

The impoundment of water by earthen dams and drilled wells, and other improvements such as fences, corrals, and ranch headquarters did not make the desert region any better grassland nor increase the rainfall or ward off the hot sunshine. The underground supply of water continues to diminish and the constant robbing of the original source of that water before it ever reaches the underground levels in the desert dooms the region to more and worse of the same.

The skin of the desert man becomes dry and hard and is more like the hide of an animal, with more wrinkles around the eyes caused by squinting at the sun and watching light-floating desert clouds.

Those of the human race who are natives of the desert and don't know any better expect less from it and suffer less from disappointments. Those who have migrated to the desert and have become trapped by its mystery and the splendors of its sunrises and the fascinating beauty of the desert sunsets ofttimes convince themselves that the desert offers great promise. Since there is well-established transportation across the semi-arid and desert regions of the Southwest, there will always be people, communications and mineral industries that will hold and support populations, but the man who intends to earn a living from the surfaces of the desert should bring himself to realize that the desert has never promised man nor animal anything but isolation and solitude, and all the rest of the brainstorms that the human race may have nurtured about promise should be evaluated rather in the light of challenge than promise, and the desert challenges man every morning when the blistering sun moves beyond that early morning grandeur.

After ten years of drouth the ingenuity of man made a very small shadow under the scorching sun, and any weeds that were colored green would have been welcome whether they were poison or sweet.

A Note About the Author

Ben K. Green, whose Horse Tradin', Some More Horse Tradin', *and* Wild Cow Tales *are already minor classics, at the very least, in a rich assemblage of Western Americana, was the kind of Westerner who almost crawled out of the cradle and into a saddle, spending his childhood, adolescence, and young manhood on horseback. He studied veterinary medicine in the United States and abroad and practiced in the Far Southwest in one of the last big horse countries in North America. When he eventually gave up his practice and research, he returned to his home town, Cumby, Texas, where, until his death in 1974, he raised good horses and cattle.*

A Note on the Type

The text of this book was set on the Linotype in a new face called Primer, designed by Rudolph Ruzicka, earlier responsible for the design of Fairfield and Fairfield Medium, Linotype faces whose virtues have for some time now been accorded wide recognition.

The complete range of sizes of Primer was first made available in 1954, although the pilot size of 12 point was ready as early as 1951. The design of the face makes general reference to Linotype Century (long a serviceable type, totally lacking in manner or frills of any kind) but brilliantly corrects the characterless quality of that face.

Typography and binding design by
Bonnie Spiegel.